The Humble Art of Journal Editing

Robert M. Davison

The Humble Art of Journal Editing

Robert M. Davison
City University of Hong Kong
Kowloon, Hong Kong

ISBN 978-3-031-52322-9   ISBN 978-3-031-52323-6 (eBook)
https://doi.org/10.1007/978-3-031-52323-6

© The Editor(s) (if applicable) and The Author(s), under exclusive license to Springer Nature Switzerland AG 2024
This work is subject to copyright. All rights are solely and exclusively licensed by the Publisher, whether the whole or part of the material is concerned, specifically the rights of translation, reprinting, reuse of illustrations, recitation, broadcasting, reproduction on microfilms or in any other physical way, and transmission or information storage and retrieval, electronic adaptation, computer software, or by similar or dissimilar methodology now known or hereafter developed.
The use of general descriptive names, registered names, trademarks, service marks, etc. in this publication does not imply, even in the absence of a specific statement, that such names are exempt from the relevant protective laws and regulations and therefore free for general use.
The publisher, the authors, and the editors are safe to assume that the advice and information in this book are believed to be true and accurate at the date of publication. Neither the publisher nor the authors or the editors give a warranty, expressed or implied, with respect to the material contained herein or for any errors or omissions that may have been made. The publisher remains neutral with regard to jurisdictional claims in published maps and institutional affiliations.

This Springer imprint is published by the registered company Springer Nature Switzerland AG
The registered company address is: Gewerbestrasse 11, 6330 Cham, Switzerland

Paper in this product is recyclable.

Acknowledgements

I gratefully acknowledge the perspicacity, wit and erudition of two close colleagues who have provided extensive commentary on an early draft: Cynthia Beath and Allen Lee. I also thank my editor at Springer, as well as the following reviewers who have seen different versions of the text: Michael Myers, Steve Alter, Monideepa Tarafdar and Andrew Burton-Jones.

I greatly appreciate the discerning and critical reflections of Kootyin that have stimulated and encouraged my humility in writing this book.

Contents

1 **Introduction** 1
   1.1 Identifying the Audience 2
   1.2 Guidelines 4
   1.3 Deconstructing the Title 6
   1.4 Organisation of the Book 8

2 **The Regular and Irregular Work Activities of Editors** 9
   2.1 Regular Activities and Communications Related to the Review Process 10
   2.2 Irregular Communications 19

3 **Cultural Values** 27
   3.1 The Editorial Advisory Board 28
   3.2 The Evolution of Cultural Values 29
   3.3 The Duty of Care for the Journal's Stakeholders 31
   3.4 Trust 33
   3.5 Integrity 34
   3.6 The Value of Time 34
   3.7 The Hazards and Delights of Diversity 35
   3.8 A Journal Is a Family 36
   3.9 Communicating the Culture 37
   3.10 Editorials and Opinions 38
   3.11 Editorial Discretions, Privileges and Consequences 42

4	**Sourcing Content and Authors**	45
	4.1 Content and Newly Established Journals	46
	4.2 Commissioning Content	47
	4.3 Sourcing Content from Conferences	48
	4.4 Sourcing via Special Issues	48
	4.5 Sourcing Excellence	51
	4.6 Sourcing Authors and Their Motivations	52
5	**Encouraging Great Reviewing Practices**	55
	5.1 Creating the Reviewing Culture and Process	56
	5.2 Characteristics of the Culture and the Reviewers	58
	5.3 Tone and Register: How to Get the Language Right	62
	5.4 Peer Review Roles	64
6	**Developing and Maintaining an Audience**	65
7	**Developing and Maintaining a Reputation**	71
8	**Engaging with the Publisher and Editorial/Production Teams**	77
9	**Continuing and Emerging Challenges and a Call to Action**	85
	9.1 Predatory Journals	85
	9.2 Plagiarism	87
	9.3 Open Access	89
	9.4 Generative AI	91
	9.5 Beyond Text: Presentation Opportunities	91
	9.6 Scanning for the Future	92
10	**Theorising Editing**	93
	10.1 Background	96
	10.2 The Editor-in-Chief's Story	98
	10.3 A Strategic Perspective on Editing	106
	10.4 Discussion	110
Appendices		113
References		133

List of Figures

Fig. 2.1	Communications and decisions for the manuscript review process (simplified)	11
Fig. 10.1	A work systems snapshot for the regular work done by the EinC	105
Fig. 10.2	A simplified balanced scorecard (BSC) (Modified from Kaplan and Norton 1992)	106
Fig. 10.3	A balanced scorecard for the EinC of an academic journal	107
Fig. 10.4	A scorecard template for the EinC of an academic journal	109

1

Introduction

Abstract This chapter provides an overview of the book, unpacking the rationale for why the book is important, explaining the title, exploring in detail who the audience may be, and outlining the structure of the book as a whole. This introduction serves as a valuable preface to the book, introducing and explaining key terms that are used throughout the book, and highlighting the key people with whom an editor needs to work.

Academic researchers disseminate their research findings in several different formats. Some prefer books, also known as monographs, or chapters in edited books. Others prefer conference proceedings. In my own field, journals are often considered to be the most prestigious venue for a researcher and so for many researchers, publishing their research in a journal is a sine qua non of academic life: they can expect to engage in this practice throughout their professional careers. The editing of academic journals is thus a key component of the research dissemination process. There are numerous journals for authors to select from, each with its own reputation and standing in a given field. Some journals publish articles[1] on a wide range of topics, but the majority occupy rather specialised niches that limit their populations of both contributing authors and readers.

Given the prevalence of research publication, the topic of academic journal editing is one that is likely to be of intrinsic interest to anyone associated with

---

[1] For the purpose of this book I refer to manuscripts published in a journal as 'articles', and to those that appear in the proceedings of a conference as 'papers'. I refer to submitted but unpublished manuscripts (for conferences and journals) as 'manuscripts', which I also abbreviate to 'ms' in diagrams.

the publication of scholarly research, whether they are editors or not. There exist many different types of journal, in terms of not just their subject matter, but also their quality, their ranking, their ownership arrangement, their business model and their culture. Some may have been recently established, whereas others may be a hundred years old or more. Some have reputations as elite or premier venues for research, whereas others are more modest in their rankings and aspirations. Given this diversity, I fully recognise the dangers associated with writing a book that purports to describe what it is that (all) journal editors do, let alone to give them advice. My account is based in very large part on my experience as the Editor in Chief (EinC) of two journals in the discipline of Information Systems (IS): the *Information Systems Journal (ISJ)*, and the *Electronic Journal of Information Systems in Developing Countries (EJISDC)*. I characterise the former as a premier and mainstream journal in the IS domain, whereas the latter is a niche journal in the same domain that caters to a more specialised audience, as implied by its name. The IS discipline itself is categorised in different ways: it is sometimes related to Computer Science or Business and Management. It can also be categorised in Library and Information Science, or as one of the Social Sciences. It is rarely considered to be an Engineering discipline, although some IS scholars do undertake engineering research. There are also niche areas in IS that are closer to Linguistics, Medicine and Law.

1.1 Identifying the Audience

In this book, I am writing for a number of different audiences. Notwithstanding my own disciplinary focus in IS, I am writing for anyone interested in the profession of academic journal editing. My descriptions and analyses are thus intended to be quite generic, i.e. they could apply to the context of any academic journal in any discipline. If I have more specific advice to give to a particular audience, e.g. newly appointed EinCs, Managing Editors (MEs), Senior Editors (SEs) or Associate Editors (AEs), then I state this clearly. I fully recognise that each individual discipline may have its own nuances and idiosyncrasies that may render my account more or less relevant. My primary audience is current and future EinCs, whether they have many years of editorial experience, have been recently appointed or are somewhere in between. As an EinC myself, I always find it valuable to listen to the opinions, stories, anecdotes and experiences of other EinCs. An infinite variety of circumstances can occur within the context of editing a journal, and learning about how such circumstances unfold, what their impacts are, and how the EinC deals with them, is always valuable. I likewise hope that this book will shed new light on some of these circumstances and thus provide food for thought for current EinCs.

My secondary audience is future EinCs, including people who are current Managing Editors (MEs), Senior Editors (SEs) or Associate Editors (AEs) in academic journals. Future EinCs, even if they have already managed special issues and conference tracks, will find that they have a lot to learn about the intricacies of editorial work. One of the anonymous reviewers of an early draft of this book commented:

> I wish I'd been able to read a book like this in 1975, after I completed my PhD, so that I could have been a better soldier in the army of people it takes to publish a journal. I think the editors I worked for assumed I understood what their challenges were, but I really had no idea. I had to learn a lot of things the hard way (or the long way). ... How many hours have all our reviewers, editors, etc spent reinventing these wheels? I'm sure there are common mistakes that we all make that could be prevented ... I wish someone had told me how to organize my reviewing and editing work, what records to keep, how to manage the time, etc.

Although I had a similar background, i.e. with experience in conference tracks, as well as in AE and SE roles in different journals, I was not particularly well prepared when I was appointed as EinC and to a considerable extent I had to undergo an extended period of what is euphemistically known as on-the-job-training, except that the training did not exist in any formal sense of the word. Instead, I was taught by (sometimes bitter) experience, and helped by many colleagues who were generous with their time.

Thirdly, I am writing for researchers who are not currently in an editorial position, but who may aspire to be one day, and who are curious about the nature of editorial work, not least because if they understood it better they might also navigate the publication process more smoothly in their role as authors. In the early years of my career, I too found the world of the journal editor to be utterly opaque. You submit your manuscript, and wait. But what happens as you wait? I hope that this book will also, inter alia, answer this and many similar questions.

Finally, I am writing for the people who oversee the work of EinCs, for instance publication or policy committees who work for the publisher, university or academic society that owns the journal. The people who serve in these important roles may never have been an EinC themselves, indeed they may not be academic researchers at all, and as a result lack detailed knowledge about the life and work of the EinC. This lack of knowledge can cause them to make poor-quality decisions, to evaluate the work of the EinC unfairly, or to fail to undertake their oversight roles adequately.

1.2 Guidelines

Much has been written about the practice and publication of research that is explicitly designed to help academics attain appropriate standards of rigour and relevance as necessary for publication, and indeed craft their research outputs in ways appropriate for different venues, notably as journal articles, conference papers, book chapters and books. These 'how to' guides are doubtless helpful, not least because they open up the black box of academic writing and make it more accessible to all academics. Examples of these types of guide include treatises about research problematisation (Alvesson and Sandberg 2011), the nature of theoretical contributions (Whetten 1989) and the role of theory in research (Díaz Andrade et al. 2023), the interestingness of research (Barney 2006) and the perspectives that researchers may take (Clarke and Davison 2020), rigour (Gioia et al. 2013), context (Davison and Martinsons 2016), literature reviews (Webster and Watson 2002), as well as countless polemical articles that seek to explain how to apply specific research methods and analytical techniques.

However, when we turn to guidelines designed to help reviewers undertake their tasks, I find that they are either very broad, for example accounts of how to write a good review, or very narrow being specific to one publishing venue and only available from the website of the venue concerned. As examples of the former, Lee (1995) and Davison et al. (2005) offer what I characterise as tutorials to the activities that reviewers perform. As examples of the latter, academic publishers like Springer[2] and Wiley[3] offer guidelines for reviewers on their websites. Thus, reviewers may be informed about basic guidelines as to their expected responsibilities and how they should structure their reviews. Reviewers who perform well may be 'promoted' to AE or SE roles, yet here too the nature of their responsibilities is seldom articulated clearly (see Tarafdar and Davison (2021) for an exception), with each person behaving more or less as they deem appropriate. Indeed, some editors behave as if their position is something to which they are entitled, scarcely fulfilling their responsibilities at all.

---

[2] https://www.springernature.com/gp/authors/campaigns/how-to-peer-review
[3] https://onlinelibrary.wiley.com/page/journal/13652575/homepage/for-reviewers

Meanwhile, guidelines explicitly written to help Editors-in-Chief (EinC) are generally absent. This book is one of a very few to address this topic.[4] It might be argued that EinCs have sufficient prior experience, gleaned through many years of reviewing as well as in SE and AE roles, but as I explain above, the circumstances that EinCs have to deal with are not only incredibly varied, but many of them far transcend the work undertaken by SEs, AEs and reviewers. Publishers may have detailed contractual terms, but these tend to focus on ensuring sufficient copy is generated in time for each issue. As we move towards continuous publication, new challenges will arise but my expectation is that EinCs will be contractually required to ensure that a certain number of articles (or perhaps journal pages) are published each year. Publishers also offer webinars and other resources to their editors,[5] yet these resources are somewhat fragmented and generic. In short, there is a dearth of detailed information that could apply to editors across a range of fields. I contend that this is a problematic situation, and one that does not give me confidence that EinCs are well-prepared for their many editorial responsibilities. I wish that, like the anonymous reviewers I cite above, when I was first appointed as an EinC there had been a book like this one that brought together the wealth of information and resources that other editors had experienced and compiled; it would have saved much reinvention of the same material. In large measure, this has been a key motivation for me to write this book.

Given the dearth of consolidated information about the nature of what being an EinC entails, and the consequent tendency for each EinC to proceed as seems idiosyncratically appropriate, it is not surprising that each journal tends to have a different set of norms, with the EinC given a more-or-less free hand in determining the standards and procedures that are followed. As a result, authors may have vastly different experiences of the review process, even at journals in the same discipline or with the same publisher. Such variance may obfuscate the purpose of research publication, i.e. to contribute to both academic knowledge and social progress.

With this situation in mind, in this book I offer a more systematic guide to what I call the 'Humble Art of Journal Editing', drawing on over two decades of experience editing two very different journals: the *ISJ*, a premier journal in its discipline and the *EJISDC*, a niche journal that caters to researchers who focus on how information systems are developed and encountered in developing countries. I will delve deeply into the nuts and bolts of editorial work, primarily as experienced by the EinC, but also with reflections on the work

---

[4] An important exception is Baruch et al. (2008)
[5] https://www.springer.com/gp/authors-editors/editors

undertaken by other editors notably SEs and AEs. It is not my intention or wish that editorial work be standardised, since each journal and editor will have their own style. However, by sharing ideas and experiences in this book I hope to inspire editors to be self-critical, to reflect on their practices, and so to raise the level of their craft, all of which should lead to better outcomes for authors, readers, reviewers and editors alike.

1.3 Deconstructing the Title

My choice of book title may provoke wry amusement or disdain: some may see journal editing as a science not an art; others may feel that my articulation positions the editors, of whom there are admittedly many fewer than authors, on a lofty pedestal so far above ordinary mortals that the book itself cannot be worth reading. Alternatively, why 'humble'? Isn't that too self-deprecatory? Aren't editors supposed to be self-aggrandising gatekeepers and custodians of their disciplines, imbued with a sense of entitlement if not downright superciliousness?! Although I accept the legitimacy of such opinions, and there are bound to be some editors like this as there are people across the human population, my intention in writing this book is to explain what it is that editors do both on a day-to-day basis and less regularly, without embellishment, but with both good humour and a sense of humility, given the enormity of the responsibility. I explicitly reject the *semper occultus* motto of spies. In contrast, I hope that this transparency will help everyone involved in the research process.

In my experience, EinCs have to be able to react to an infinite variety of circumstances that may occur. Although the daily routine is predictable, there are many other non-routine activities that are not in the least bit predictable. Thus, a simple template for daily activities would only be useful to some degree. Many other activities will fall under the heading 'Others'. Thus, while guidelines are always helpful, extraordinary circumstances require extraordinary measures where the EinC must create an immediate response or solution. Almost any illustrative example that I provide could be labelled as 'extreme', yet all the examples, stories and anecdotes in this book are essentially real. I modified examples in a few cases so as to preserve the anonymity and dignity of the people or journals concerned, but none of the content was concocted or contrived to fit a need and I did not use a generative AI programme to create text at any stage.

As an example of an occasional circumstance, consider the proposer of a special issue who displays self-righteous indignation at my rejection of his proposal and persists on sending multiple follow-up emails demanding that I change my mind. It later turns out that he has done the same with multiple other journal editors, all of whom have rejected his proposal. Or the author of an accepted manuscript who refuses to sign the copyright transfer agreement and essentially withdraws her manuscript from publication. Later I find out that her action was instigated by her dean who thinks that the journal is not good enough and she can do better elsewhere. These are but two of the many occasional circumstances that can occur. They are essentially unpredictable, may never be repeated in the same form, yet cannot be ignored. The editor must formulate a response in each case. For the record, in the first case, having explained the circumstances of the rejection with great care but to no avail, I referred the proposer to the publisher, with a detailed cover note of my own. In the second, I discussed with the publisher, who wrote to the dean to object to his behaviour, and at the same time stored the names of both the author and the dean in my memory. They are still there, 20 years later.

EinCs need to develop the knack of knowing how to respond to each situation, yet must also have the humility to recognise their imperfections and to invite their SEs and AEs to support them. Balancing these competing pressures and constraints effectively and fairly, recognising where one has fallen short and where there are opportunities for improvement, is an art. A good EinC, in my view, is a constant student, a life-long learner: if nothing else, the EinC is a witness of the full panoply of human foibles. I suggest that EinCs who have developed the ability to steer their journals through the many minefields that pop-up will enhance their journals' reputation and, in the process, garner considerable respect. As the title also suggests, a dose of humility is also important. It can greatly enhance communication effectiveness. Throughout this book, I will highlight both the 'art' of journal editing and the element of 'humility' that I believe is essential to the consummate editor.

In addition to these motives for writing this book, by offering insights into how editors think and what they expect, as well as by sharing their experiences, it is my hope that researchers will be able to position their research more effectively and thus enhance the likelihood that their manuscripts will be accepted for publication. Meanwhile, reviewers may achieve a deeper understanding of how the review process is managed, which may be valuable should they be offered an AE or SE position. Meanwhile, current SEs and AEs, especially those who aspire to be an EinC one day, will understand better the nature of their role and some of the challenges that EinCs face. In my view, everyone involved in the review process, but especially EinCs, SEs and AEs, should be humble, given their responsibilities and power to determine the fate of submitted academic research manuscripts, and vicariously their authors. Writing this book, and reading and responding to the feedback of many friends and colleagues, has itself been a humbling experience.

1.4 Organisation of the Book

The book is organised as follows: following this introduction (Chap. 1), I first examine what editors actually do on a more or less regular basis (Chap. 2), before continuing to examine how editors may promulgate the cultural values of academic journals (Chap. 3). Next (Chap. 4), I examine the many issues associated with sourcing content, including the different types of manuscript that can be submitted. From the publisher's perspective this is perhaps the major responsibility of editors. I consider the novelty of research, and its breadth and depth. I also make the case for indigenous theorisation, serendipity, iconoclastic research and the potential of special issues. In Chap. 5, I deal with the review process and suggest how editors may formulate effective guidelines for reviewers that lead to constructive/developmental advice for authors. Here I also deal with the diversity of editorial review boards and the different roles played by SEs and AEs. The audience of the journal deserves attention (Chap. 6) since published research needs to meet their needs and expectations, which are likely to shift over time. A long-term perspective is essential to the continued thriving of a journal, which means that editors must seek to develop and maintain the journal's reputation (Chap. 7). Editors also need to establish and maintain a close working relationship with their publisher (Chap. 8), including production and copyediting teams. Here, there is the potential for conflict given the different drivers of 'excellence': editors may prefer a lower acceptance rate, and a higher impact factor, so as to demonstrate quality, yet the publisher will also have a financial viability and contribution perspective that cannot be ignored. In Chap. 9, I highlight some continuing and emerging challenges, such as ChatGPT and other generative AI tools, predatory journals, and the open access movement. In the last chapter (Chap. 10), I take a very different stance and attempt to theorise what it is that editors do. This draws on some of my own prior empirical research and functions as a stand-alone essay on the various influences on and characteristics of the editor at work. The suggestion to write this chapter came from Allen Lee, who asked me to shun the native editor perspective and instead to imagine myself as an Anthropologist, studying what it is that editors do, and crafting a theory to explain it. The chapter allows me to bring in more of my personal thoughts about the nature of editorial work and so closes the book, though there is a list of selected references and several Appendices with additional materials.

2

The Regular and Irregular Work Activities of Editors

Abstract This chapter is structured around a description of the more or less regular daily activities of editors. These include communications with a wide variety of stakeholders, predominantly associated with the handling of manuscripts and the decisions reached thereon. Insights here will be of interest to researchers in particular since they are often the people most directly affected by the decisions.

The EinC of an academic journal has a number of competing prerogatives to attend to, each of which has the potential to consume considerable time and energy. Some of these activities, for instance those relating to the managing of submitted manuscripts, are quotidian: they take place more or less every day. Other activities are more irregular: they could happen at any time. This latter group includes communications with a variety of different stakeholders. Finally, there are activities that rarely happen yet may require some ingenuity to deal with. The cumulative effect of these various activities can be overwhelming at times: I've been in situations where there are 20 new submissions that need to be screened and then assigned to SEs, as well as ten reviewed submissions that need a decision. On top of this, there may be complaints from authors, concerns from SEs, questions from the publisher, requests from authors for feedback as to the potential suitability of a manuscript for the journal. EinCs also have a life beyond the journal, with their own research, teaching and various service activities, not to mention a family and anything else.

Do editors get time off? Holidays? Do they stop being an editor for a few weeks a year? They could, but if they do then when they return they will find perhaps 100 tasks waiting for them, not to mention irate authors, absent reviewers, and worse. It may be possible to appoint an interim EinC when the EinC is away, at least to handle the more mundane activities, but we can't expect the world to stop. Meanwhile, SEs and AEs can indicate that they will be unavailable for a period of time, and hence prefer not to receive new manuscripts to handle, but the manuscripts that they handled previously may come back after revision and so will need their attention sooner or later. Authors keep writing and submitting manuscripts all the time, while decisions need to be reached more or less continually. A delay of more than a few days is likely to lead to a significant build-up of work.

Given these competing demands, it is all too easy for the EinC to be dictatorial, putting humility aside in favour of brief, direct and robust communications that are certainly unequivocal, yet that may also significantly annoy their interlocutors. Despite the pressure to complete a multitude of tasks I suggest that a dose of humility is still very helpful. Editors at all levels are servants of a review and publication process. Their task is to ensure fairness, equitable treatment and just decisions. They need to be polite, constructive, developmental, and encouraging in their feedback to authors, reviewers and everyone else even in the most difficult and contrary of situations, and when faced with the most intractable and obnoxious individuals. They also need to communicate with a variety of other stakeholders, including: members of the editorial board, prospective authors, and members of the production and publication teams.

2.1 Regular Activities and Communications Related to the Review Process

In recent years, I have found that while the volume of submissions to journals has swollen dramatically, the willingness of scholars to undertake high-quality reviews has not kept track. Some EinCs have tried mandating the undertaking of reviews as a condition of submission, i.e. when you submit your manuscript you agree to review X manuscripts for the same journal. This makes sense in principle, and it works well if these author-reviewers take their tasks seriously. But in practice the quality of these coerced reviews varies markedly and I now find that quality cannot be conscripted in this way. Volunteer reviewers tend to produce better quality reviews, largely I think because they are motivated to do so, recognising both the importance of the peer review process and the value that they can get for themselves through their service.

2 The Regular and Irregular Work Activities of Editors

On the other hand, I have also had conversations with authors who glibly told me that while they submit manuscripts, they never review for any journal; I suppose that this has the merit of honesty but I regard it as utterly selfish behaviour that constitutes an abuse of the peer review system. The system works if everyone who submits also undertakes reviews, ideally at least two reviews per submission since each submission requires at least two reviewers. As an EinC of two journals, I could argue that I can't be a reviewer as well, but since I write and submit research manuscripts, which need to be reviewed, I feel obliged to review too, at least for the journals and conferences to which I submit.

Given the imbalance between the volume of submissions and the lack of willing reviewers, many editors must therefore attempt to ensure that only the submissions that have a good chance of surviving the review process are sent for review. Reaching and communicating decisions about submitted manuscripts constitute the single most significant part of an EinC's daily work. At the two journals where I am an EinC, we accept 8–12% of submissions. Across the two journals, we receive in total around 1000 submissions annually. Each submission requires between 1 and perhaps 30 communications (with the authors, SE and AE, and reviewers) before a final decision is reached.

Figure 2.1 provides a simplified overview of the process flow and communications, while a text description of the process (including more examples and exceptions) follows. I must note here that the model and description below is neither the only model nor a preferred model. Journals vary markedly in their editorial architectures. While most will have an EinC (and a few have

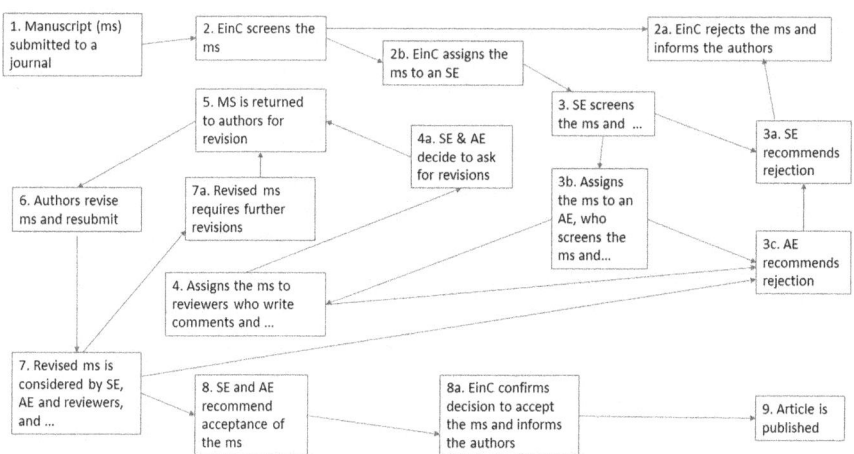

Fig. 2.1 Communications and decisions for the manuscript review process (simplified)

multiple simultaneous EinCs), some both have SEs and AEs, others have either SEs or AEs but not both, and a few may have neither SEs nor AEs, i.e. the EinC assigns manuscripts to reviewers directly, greatly simplifying communications. Some journals have established formal editorial review boards (ERB) with a brigade of longer-term reviewers, whereas other journals have no ERB at all and locate reviewers for each manuscript on an ad hoc basis. There are even models that do not require any kind of EinC involvement, i.e. only peer reviewers are involved, with an editorial assistant (EA) to coordinate. Some journals have departments or sections, headed by an editor who may be free to act autonomously, i.e. with respect to the decisions made. At some journals, the EinC can change the architecture but at others they are bound by it and have very limited freedom to innovate.

When an author submits a manuscript to a journal (1), it is first checked by an editorial assistant (EA). I provide a detailed description of the EA's responsibilities in Chap. 8. The checking covers plagiarism (using iThenticate), generative AI (i.e. does the manuscript appear to be written using a generative AI programme like ChatGPT), submission requirements and formatting standards, but the checking typically does not extend to content suitability. If the formatting is incorrect, the EA requests the author(s) to modify and resubmit. The nature of what kind of format is required varies considerably from journal to journal. For instance, some journals allow free style formatting where the authors can format however they like, so long as they are consistent. Other journals have very strict protocols that are enforced by the EA. For instance, authors may fail to: remove information that identifies them from the main text; provide an abstract and keywords; include a cover letter; provide the necessary meta-data, e.g. email addresses and affiliations for all co-authors; format the document in a single column or the references following APA standards. These formatting and submission errors need to be fixed before the manuscript can be assigned to the EinC. An example of text from an EA letter to an author follows:

> Firstly, a Title Page should be submitted that contains: title of manuscript, suggested running headline of not more than 45 characters including spaces, followed by the author's name, department, institution, city, country and number of words. This should be uploaded as a separate document, under file type 'Title Page'. Secondly, the title page in your Main Document should be without the author details to facilitate 'blind' refereeing.

Some of these requirements may seem picky or unduly onerous and it is true that they can be deterministic. What if you don't have an affiliation (perhaps you are retired or unemployed)? What if you don't live in a city but in a village? While there are exceptions, most of the time the requirements can be met and the EinC can always override them if necessary.

If the iThenticate similarity score is high (indicating an unacceptable level of self-plagiarism or uncited sources), the EA informs the EinC. Usually it is the EinC who asks the authors to revise the text to lower the iThenticate score. Some EinCs specify that the similarity score must be no higher than 10%. Other EinCs are less strict, but any score over 30% is likely to raise concerns. If a manuscript contains material that is copied from a PhD thesis, which is not subject to copyright restrictions, then a high score may be less concerning. If a manuscript is derived from a conference paper that has not been (extensively) modified, then a high score may result. Some journals allow such submissions, the thinking being that during the revision process the text will likely change significantly and so the similarity score will fall. Other journals do not allow such high levels of similarity, no matter the circumstances, and so may require substantial editing before the manuscript can enter the review process.

If the manuscript appears to be significantly authored with a generative AI programme, the EA informs the EinC, but a reject is highly likely unless the journal explicitly permits the use of generative AI. I discuss this in more detail in Chap. 8. Once the EA is satisfied with the format of the submitted manuscript, it is assigned to the EinC. The EinC can make a number of different decisions with regard to the submitted manuscript. Each decision comes with an accompanying logic that is reflected in the text that accompanies the decision in the communication that is sent to the author.

The EinC's first task is to screen (2) the manuscript for quality, suitability and fit with the journal. This screening can also be delegated to a Managing Editor (ME), who should be a disciplinary expert. If a journal's field of coverage is extensive, it may be necessary for multiple MEs to be appointed, each responsible for a different topic area. This screening is not the same as reading the whole manuscript thoroughly. Instead, it is a first-cut attempt to gauge if the manuscript is in scope and has a chance of surviving the review process. If the manuscript is either out of scope or unsuitable for whatever reason, the manuscript is immediately desk rejected (2a). This desk reject decision is final: authors are not permitted to revise and resubmit it to the same journal. However, some authors attempt to negotiate the desk rejection, for instance by highlighting some important feature that the EinC or ME may have missed and so requesting a re-evaluation. Although the EinC should take note of the appeal, it is highly unlikely to be successful if the screening process has been handled correctly.

Some authors are polite to a fault, even when their manuscripts are rejected, writing to appreciate the constructive feedback that they received, generously offering to help the journal by contributing future reviews, and indicating that they will submit manuscripts in the future. It is a pleasure to read these epistles, because I realise that our hard work in handling the review process has been appreciated, even if the outcome is not favourable. Here is an example of such a reply received from authors after their manuscript was rejected:

> On behalf of my co-authors including myself, we like to thank you, the senior editor, associate editor and two reviewers in providing insightful comments when reviewing our manuscript for publication. We are very grateful for the details they provided that will help with improving our manuscript.
>
> While we were hoping for a more positive outcome, we will take these comments suggested here and revise our manuscript meticulously. Writing a manuscript for publication is a journey and the much-improved manuscript through these careful revisions will be accepted in another journal.

Unfortunately, the reverse situation also occurs: some authors are unable to accept a reject decision, no matter how politely it is conveyed, and resort to vitriolic attack, threatening to sue the editor and the publisher for defamation of character (by not accepting the manuscript unmodified). These unhappy authors are particularly sensitive to the language used in the editorial decision. I've learned that it is better not to use dismissive or trivialising language and say things like 'I skimmed through your manuscript' or even 'Based on my initial screening of your manuscript' because of the opportunity for misinterpretation. It's much safer, and not significantly more onerous, to be respectful and to observe 'I have read your manuscript carefully. It addresses an important question/topic/problem which is inherently worth investigating. However, …'. Perhaps this is no more than insincere flattery, but if it serves to reduce tensions and does not involve the telling of lies, I see no good reason not to be a little more gentle. In contrast, an abrupt or dismissive communication is less likely to be appreciated. No one wants to be told that they've been wasting their time (even if it's true) on a research project that really should be shredded and thrown to the winds.

Authors expect that their manuscripts, which may represent considerable investment of money (to undertake the research) and time (to conduct and later write up the research), will be read with care and given due appreciation. They expect to see detailed feedback that, even if not adulatory, provides detailed constructive advice as to how they can improve their work leading to publication in the journal. If authors react violently, I find it is better not to respond immediately at all but to let the situation calm down first. If I do reply, it is always to explain the nature of the screening and reviewing process, and to repeat the reasons for the decision.

I am careful not to add new information relating to the substance of the reason why the manuscript is rejected. I do not add new information because I don't want to add fuel to the fire in the author's mind and I don't want to provide the author with more things to disagree with. I always cc the publisher when I reply to these angry messages, so that the authors know (a) that the publisher is involved and (b) who the publishing contact is, in case the author wants to contact the publisher directly.

I recall a situation when I rejected a manuscript that appeared to have four authors. It later turned out that the first was a PhD student who was the submitting author, the second was the supervisor, and the third and fourth were 'famous' people. The reject letter went to all four, and all four complained, though for different reasons. The first author loudly complained that I could not reject the manuscript because the (other) authors were so famous! The second, third and fourth authors complained that they had never written such a manuscript, let alone submitted it. When I explained the situation, the second said that he would 'talk' to the student, while the third and fourth asked to see the submission that they had not written yet were apparently authors of, and later apologised for their inadvertent non-role in the situation. The first author never got back to me.

Assuming that a submitted manuscript passes the EinC's (or ME's) initial screening, the EinC assigns it to an appropriately qualified SE (2b) who undertakes a second screening (3). The SE is almost invariably an expert with respect to some aspect of the manuscript (method, topic, theory, epistemology) and therefore well-placed to assess the manuscript and its merits. The SE also has the prerogative to reject at this time (3a), but if it is screened positively then the SE assigns it to an AE (3b) who also screens the manuscript. The SE and AE habitually communicate (by email) about the manuscript. If the AE argues that it should be rejected at this stage (3c), then the manuscript returns to the SE who (normally) confirms the rejection (3a) and the manuscript is then channelled to the EinC who (normally) confirms the rejection (2a). I say 'normally' because there are exceptions and at any stage a different outcome might eventuate, e.g. if the SE thinks that the AE is too harsh, in which case the SE might choose to assign a new AE.

If the AE and SE agree that the manuscript has the potential to survive the review process, then the SE and AE work together to identify potential reviewers (including those that the authors may have nominated, but being mindful of conflicts of interest that may exist) and contact them (4) to seek their agreement to review by a certain deadline. Assuming that the identified reviewers agree to review, they are formally invited (normally by the AE) to be reviewers in the manuscript management system (MMS) that is used to manage the review process. The system then makes both the manuscript and the review forms available to the authors. As the deadline for completion of the reviews approaches, or passes, either the system (automatically) or the AE (manually) will contact the reviewers and encourage them to submit their reviews by the deadline, or as soon as possible. When reviews have been delivered, the SE and AE independently write up reports that incorporate both their own assessments of the manuscript and those of the reviewers. The SE and AE may recommend that the manuscript be (4a) revised, (3c/3a) rejected, or (8) accepted. Accepting a manuscript after a single round of review, i.e. without revisions, is extremely unusual. The actual communication with the authors, which is almost invariably by email embedded in the MMS, may be sent by the SE or the EinC, depending on the journal's normal protocols. At some journals, it is the EinC who formally communicates decisions. At other journals, the SEs may be given this prerogative and the EinC only intervenes in exceptional cases. If the SE, AE and reviewers are consistent in their recommendation, then it is usually the case that the EinC endorses their view, whether to accept, revise or reject the manuscript. If the SE, AE and reviewers are split in their recommendations, then the EinC needs to pay more careful attention to the circumstances, but in practice it is highly unusual for the EinC to disagree with the SE's recommendation.

An example of a situation where I did disagree with the SE (and the rest of the review team) was one where there were multiple conflicts of interest between authors, reviewers, AE and SE. As a result, I felt that the review process had not been handled appropriately and it was better to start again. Although the whole review team recommended acceptance, I instead assigned the most recent submission to a new SE and explained the circumstances. With a new review team in place, a very different set of recommendations emerged and the manuscript was eventually rejected. I had to explain this very carefully to the author team which, fortunately, did not demur. Meanwhile, I also had to explain the situation and outcome to the former review team. This was not an easy communication and it led to the former SE and AE stepping down from their roles at the journal.

Having received the invitation to revise (5), the authors then revise the manuscript (6) and resubmit it to the journal, where it will be reconsidered (7) by the SE first, the AE second and finally the reviewers. If the SE is satisfied with the revisions, it may be accepted at that point (8), or after the AE's agreement, or after the entire review team has had a chance to evaluate the revised manuscript. The EinC then confirms the acceptance (8a) and sends the formal notification to the authors (9). Alternatively, the manuscript may be returned to the authors for further revisions (7a). In later rounds of the review process, it may not be necessary to involve the reviewers at all, i.e. the SE and AE can reach a decision on the outcome by themselves. At the journals I edit, published articles have typically gone through four review-revise cycles, though some might be accepted after 1–2 revision cycles and a few might need 5–6 revision cycles. Manuscripts can be rejected at any stage, but where possible I prefer to reject earlier not later, so as to conserve reviewer and author resources. If a manuscript is not making progress towards acceptance, I think it is better to reject it earlier rather than string the authors out with a series of major revisions that never lead to a satisfactory conclusion.

In most peer-review models, while reviewers and the AE all have the responsibility to offer an opinion and make a recommendation, they are not strictly deciding or even voting. The prerogative to decide the fate of the manuscript rests with the person who communicates the decision (whether the SE or the EinC). This decision is usually consistent with the review team's opinions, but there can be many good reasons for inconsistency. For instance, the review team may be split with some reviewers suggesting the manuscript be rejected while others think that the authors should be given the opportunity to revise it. Furthermore, the AE and SE may disagree with each other. Even when the whole review team has reached consensus, the SE or EinC has the prerogative to reach a final decision. For instance, it could be that the review team recommends rejection, but the SE or EinC decides to be more lenient and offers a reject and resubmit decision. Alternatively, the review team may recommend acceptance, yet the SE or EinC may be unconvinced and decide that the manuscript should be revised further or even rejected.

The EinC does not take these decisions lightly, often communicating with the SE, especially in controversial situations. For instance, the EinC and SE may schedule a zoom call to work out the details. But the EinC is the only person who is contractually obliged to the publisher and thus is the only person who is strictly accountable for the research that is accepted for publication. EinCs and SEs may choose to give precise instructions to authors, beyond those offered by the AE and reviewers, if they ask them to revise the manuscript, for instance explaining that some of the comments made by the review team are more important, or that others need not be addressed at all. SEs need to take care that the reviews are not contradictory, or if they are that clear guidance is provided to the authors to ensure that they know how to revise the manuscript.

Sometimes, an AE or SE may find that reviewer comments are incomprehensible (poor use of language, grammatical and syntax errors), unreasonably biased, impolite, aggressive, or insulting. In this situation, the AE/SE may rescind the review, i.e. send it back to the reviewer for revision, ideally with a clear explanation of the problem. Normally, the reviewer is willing to change the text and the revised review can then be incorporated into the decision letter. However, some reviewers refuse to change their text. I recall one reviewer who said 'Well, it's obvious what I mean so even though there may be spelling mistakes I refuse to fix them'. If this happens, the AE can either decide not to use the review at all, essentially discarding it, or can proceed to include the review. In either case, it is sensible for the AE to let the SE know about the situation. It is important to note that in the journals I edit, AEs are not permitted to edit reviews so as to remove, add or modify material. However, I am aware that in other journals AEs almost routinely edit reviewer comments. If an SE has a problem with an AE report, then the SE can also rescind it and request changes. If the AE refuses to change, this creates an impasse that can be hard to resolve. In principle, the SE can remove the AE (without affecting the reviews) and either assign a new (different) AE or perform the AE work directly (i.e. the SE and AE are the same person). The SE should certainly inform the EinC about such a situation as the AE may well complain about the SE's behaviour to the EinC. The EinC can also rescind an SE report: I did so recently when the SE made a simple yet obvious and critical mistake in her SE report. She asked for major revisions but indicated that she could *not* see a path to publication. The contradiction of the two terms was at best confusing and therefore needed resolution prior to communication with the authors. Fortunately, she agreed with me and revised her recommendation accordingly. This demonstrates that EinCs need to read the SE, AE and reviewer reports carefully before sending them to the authors.

A regular task for me is to help the SE or AE do something that they can do by themselves yet don't know how, or have forgotten. For instance, an SE may want to change the AE on a manuscript. In principle, this is not difficult, yet if you don't know how then it is impossible. Meanwhile, the AE may want to make a decision without involving reviewers. The default option in the MMS is for two reviewers to be appointed, so the AE has to change this setting to zero reviewers, but again if the AE doesn't know how to do this, the EinC has to step in and help. In a recent example, the SE told me that an AE had been assigned to the manuscript, yet the AE could not find the manuscript when he logged in. This sounds like a system bug, but it's actually more simple. What happened was that the AE had three different accounts on the MMS, each with a different email address. The AE had forgotten about two of them and only used the third, but the SE had assigned to one of the forgotten ones. I then had to merge the three accounts into one: this caused all the details of all three accounts to be merged, including manuscripts handled as AE or reviewer, manuscripts submitted as author, etc. I set as the primary account the one that had the AE status. This resolved the problem. The AE could then log into this one account and change details as needed. What this implies is that the EinC must be an expert in the MMS, must have administrative privileges, and must be able to resolve any of these fairly mundane issues quickly. Of course, it is always possible to ask the EA for help, but I find that the EA may take up to a week to resolve problems which is often too long to wait.

I am aware that at some journals, the EA protects their prerogative to be the only person permitted to handle the back-office functions of the MMS, even though they may be off work (sick, on holiday or otherwise incapacitated) for weeks at a time with no one to cover them with the result that submitted manuscripts pile up and authors wonder what's happening. The EinC needs to handle this kind of situation with sensitivity, to protect the prerogative of the EA but also to enact the duty of care that is owed to authors, reviewers and all other stakeholders. Clearly the reputation of a journal may be damaged when any key stakeholder (be it EinC, EA, reviewer or author) fails to undertake work to the best of their professional ability. Since the performance of the EinC may be negatively assessed by these events beyond the EinC's control, it is very much in the EinC's interest to intervene in the MMS as necessary, even if this means stepping over the notional role boundaries and trespassing on the role prerogatives of other actors, such as the EA.

Occasionally, it happens that a reviewer, AE, SE or EinC passes away or is somehow incapacitated and is unable to perform his/her duties for an extended period of time. In each case, a new person must be assigned to the role. If the individual was responsible for reviews of multiple manuscripts, or was handling multiple manuscripts as AE or SE, then all of those manuscripts will need to be reassigned. If the EinC passes away, a new EinC will have to be appointed at short notice, yet there is little opportunity to pass on duties to the new incumbent and much long-established knowledge about the journal may be lost. I deal with this situation in more detail in Chap. 7.

2.2 Irregular Communications

Apart from these email communications with authors, reviewers and editors, which are a normal part of the review process, the EinC will also need to engage on an occasional basis with a variety of other people for a wide range of purposes: prospective authors, prospective special issue editors, manuscript agencies, current and prospective SEs and AEs, the editors of other journals, and the publication and production teams of the journal.

Some prospective authors write to request pre-submission feedback on their manuscripts. This could be quite a time-taking activity and it's not entirely fair for them to expect a detailed pre-submission report. I generally limit myself to a couple of lines to indicate the general suitability of the material for the journal. Some prospective authors write to ask for information about the journal, for instance its pricing policy, or how long they need to wait for reviews. Much of this information is available on the journal's website, but a quick answer, often with links to the relevant webpages, is needed.

Sadly, some authors resort to what I would characterise as emotional blackmail. For instance, they observe that in order to keep their job, get promoted, or graduate, they need to have a manuscript accepted by a specific date (often a mere few days later) and so would I be so kind as to confirm that I will accept their manuscript as soon as they submit it, i.e. essentially without review. Sometimes financial incentives are offered, i.e. personal payments to my bank account. Agencies that claim to represent authors write to ask if I can guarantee to publish a certain number of manuscripts without review, with a payment to me to facilitate this process.

To all these kinds of enquiries, I repeat what is already on the website, that any author is welcome to submit, that we have no submission or publication charges (though you can pay for open access if you wish), and that all manuscripts are reviewed before a decision is reached. I indicate the journal's current accept rate and point out that accepted manuscripts typically go through Y rounds of review before acceptance, a process that typically takes Z months. These are very much standard communications, for which I maintain templates (see Appendix A) to ensure consistency, but my fundamental principle is that I need to respond as politely as I can to each person who writes, no matter how trivial, ridiculous, rebarbative or unnecessary the question.

For instance, I was recently contacted by a prospective buyer of one of the journals that I edit! Fortunately, I don't own the journals, so I can't sell them, but the same individual contacted me repeatedly, despite my repeated insistence that I could not sell the journal. As this person wrote:

> 'I'm sorry to bother you. I'm Doctor T from the Hunan University. I learned from the official website of "Information Systems Journal" that you are the editor of the journal. Is your journal for sale? Or do you know of any journals that are up for sale? If your magazine is willing to sell, my team is willing to buy it.

If it is convenient, can I add your wechat or WhatsApp? You can contact me at any time. I wish you good health and a happy life'.

What I try very hard not to do is to get into a protracted conversation or discussion with the people who write. For instance, some of these interlocutors seem to take pleasure in criticising journal or publisher policy, and try to provoke me into either a defence of the policy or a commitment to change the policy. Others ask if I can mentor them and provide feedback on any topic they ask about. I understand that EinCs may be seen to be influential or seasoned scholars whose regular advice could be valuable, but if I agree to mentor one then to be fair I should do so for anyone who asks, which is not feasible.

I receive a lot of proposals to publish a special issue in the journals I edit. During the course of writing this chapter, I received five such proposals in two days! We have detailed guidelines for special issue proposals, though looking at some of the proposals I am not sure that these guidelines are read. My initial screening of a special issue proposal leads to one of two outcomes. If the proposal is well written, within scope for the journal, has a sensible time frame and proposed guest editors who are respected scholars with a reputation in the topic area, I normally send the proposal to the journal's SEs and AEs to solicit feedback. Specifically, I ask them to evaluate the proposal itself, to suggest revisions, and to indicate if they would be interested in serving alongside the proposed guest editors in an editorial role. I send their feedback, as well as my own, to the proposed guest editors and request a revision. This proposal review-revision process will iterate 2–3 times until a clearly articulated and focused version emerges that can be quickly converted into a call for submissions. I arrange for this call for submissions to appear on the journal's website and the confirmed guest editors promote the special issue. In all cases, I (as EinC) serve as the ME for the special issue. This means that I handle all communications with authors, but I do not actively play a role in the reviewing of manuscripts or the reaching of decisions: these are the responsibilities of the special issue guest SEs.

If, in contrast, the proposal is unsuitable, I reject it with a quick email to the special issue proposer. Common reasons for unsuitability are: the topic is too technical or narrow; the proposed guest editors lack sufficient experience in the domain of the journal (indeed, they often have no experience at all); and the proposed time frame from submission to publication is too short with no more than one round of review and revision possible. Most of these putative special issue editors never respond to the rejection: presumably they try elsewhere. But occasionally I get a very angry response along the lines of 'how dare you query my qualifications or expertise. I demand the right to edit a special issue in your journal'. I respond as politely as I can but if this fails I refer the individual to the publisher. I discuss special issues in more detail in Chap. 4.

Successful EinCs are supported by a large team of SEs and AEs. It would not be unusual to see anything up to 50 or even 100 SEs and AEs at journals with large numbers of submissions. Developing the SE and AE team is a critical component of the EinC's responsibilities. By 'developing' I mean providing opportunities for professional growth and skill acquisition. I expect that SEs and AEs will communicate with each other about the manuscripts that they handle, including the identification of potential reviewers, since this communication should lead to a more sophisticated understanding of the strengths and weaknesses of the manuscript, and how the manuscript can most effectively be reviewed. When a decision is reached, we routinely share the entire review packet (SE and AE reports and individual reviews) with the entire review team. This provides an invaluable opportunity for the AE to learn from the SE's rationale for the decision, as well as for the reviewers to learn how both the other reviewers engaged with the manuscript and how the SE and AE reached their respective decisions. I try to assign manuscripts to SEs and AEs that fit within their current areas of competence. I maintain a document that lists all SE and AE keywords, i.e. reflecting their competence, and share this information with all SEs. However, sometimes it is not possible to assign manuscripts that are within the keyword comfort zone and so occasionally SEs and AEs may be asked to handle a manuscript that is epistemologically, methodologically or topically unfamiliar. This too can be a learning opportunity since other members of the review team, notably the reviewers, should be experts.

In considering new SE and AE appointments, my fundamental principle is that we should appoint SEs from the best of the AEs. Here 'best' references such attributes as: high-quality work; adherence to deadlines; willingness to engage with the journal's activities, such as contributing ideas to editorials, collaborating on special issues, participating in author-mentoring and manuscript-writing workshops that we organise during conferences; willingness to handle manuscripts from outside the self-defined comfort zone. Meanwhile, we appoint AEs from the best of the reviewers, focusing on those who consistently write high-quality reviews that are submitted on time. AEs can also be appointed from the population of special issue guest editors who have completed their special issue on time and demonstrated an appropriate degree of care for submitting authors, reviewers, editors and the journal's own audience. Towards the end of each calendar year, I invite current SEs and AEs to nominate candidates for consideration as future SEs and AEs. I require evidence for these nominations (along the lines indicated above) as well as the curriculum vitae of the individual person concerned for AE appointments. Self-nomination for an AE or SE position is also possible, though in practice, very few such unsolicited nominations lead to appointments. When I check their records, most are quite opportunistic and few have published in or reviewed for the journal that they hope to be associated with; indeed, they may not have even published in the same discipline. Nevertheless, occasionally we do identify a star AE or SE in this way and I am grateful that they alerted us to their willingness to serve.

The duration of an SE or AE appointment varies considerably. At some journals, it is two or three years, but four or even five at others. Some journals allow multiple extensions of the appointment, but others only allow a single extension. Equally, early curtailment of an appointment is also possible if there are problems. At some journals, the entire cohort of SEs and AEs serves in parallel with the term of the EinC, i.e. a new EinC brings in an entire new team and the old team steps down. Occasionally SEs and AEs choose to step down because they realise that they don't have the time to do a good job, or for other reasons. For instance, an AE recently stepped down because he objected to providing unpaid labour to a commercial publisher. I address this issue in Chap. 8. If SEs or AEs have editorial commitments at other journals then they may find that they are overloaded, and need to step down. Other overload situations may be more temporary, e.g. the person has new administrative responsibilities at work, is on maternity or paternity leave, or has to care for a family member. In these cases, I grant what amounts to a sabbatical from journal work. Such sabbaticals tend to be individually negotiated rather than automated: there may be a need for a break for a few weeks or months or even a couple of years. If it seems likely that the break will be substantial, it may be better to consider asking the SE or AE to step down altogether.

Very rarely, I need to ask an SE or AE to step down. This is usually because of a failure to commit sufficient time to the journal, with the result that the completion of tasks is long (months) overdue and communications are sporadic at best. Asking a person to step down is not pleasant, but the EinC cannot shirk this responsibility. Here, 'step down' is clearly a euphemism for dismissal, and the decision is generally final, though it is better to try and engage the individual in a conversation about the situation long before that decision is reached. An even more remote reason for the SE or AE to be removed is when the individual becomes late. In such situations, the EinC has to make arrangements for all the manuscripts currently being handled by the individual concerned. Often these involve delayed actions (to assign a manuscript to an AE or reviewer, to make a decision following reviews) and so other people (SEs or AEs) need to be found to take on the extra work at short notice.

From time to time I write to the current SEs and AEs about topics important to the journal. These may involve new policy directions, invitations to participate in a workshop or to attend an editorial board meeting. I regard these communications as essential. As I explain in the next chapter, as editor one of my key purposes is to develop a strong culture at the journals I edit. I maintain regular contact with all the SEs and AEs as a group, as well as individually, and seek to develop a sense of 'family' among them. When their reports are delayed, I need to remind them. When they deliver exceptionally good reports, I thank them personally. I create opportunities for them to be more deeply involved in journal activities, for instance in special issues and other policy matters, as well as at conferences where they may represent the journal on a 'meet the editors' panel or perhaps run a workshop that focuses on the development of manuscripts for later submission to the journal.

The EinCs of journals in the same discipline keep in quite close contact with each other. We do not see ourselves as competitors or rivals: on the contrary, we are allies. I am grateful that the editors of other journals have provided pre-publication feedback on this book. We share experiences, problems and solutions. We participate in panels at conferences. My view is that each journal has (or should have) its own niche and culture, and thus should not be competing with the other journals for author attention or submissions. A manuscript that is written for one journal is unlikely to be suitable for another journal without modification. Thus, I see no harm but a lot of benefit from these inter-editor conversations. At the same time, journals in the same field may compete with each other for the people who serve in SE and AE roles. At the *ISJ* we have no policy about this currently, i.e. any SE or AE is free to serve in the same or a different role at any other journal according to preference. However, I am aware of some journals where as a matter of policy, people are excluded from working at any other journal or at more than a fixed number of other journals or at a specific journal that is seen as a competitor.

Unfortunately, EinCs also need to keep in touch in situations where there are ethical issues at stake. Occasionally authors may submit the same manuscript to multiple journals simultaneously. Although I can understand the author perspective, i.e. of maximising the chance of acceptance, from an editorial perspective it is a waste of resources and a violation of the code of ethics of many academic communities. If the manuscript was accepted by both journals, the author could not sign a copyright transfer for both and would thus have to withdraw the manuscript from one, essentially wasting all the resources that that journal had already committed to the review process. If such double submission is detected, the editors of the two journals need to communicate so as to reach an agreed solution: normally both editors reject the manuscript, irrespective of the merits of the manuscript itself. They may take further action by alerting their respective publishers and even contacting the institution where the author(s) work(s).

For instance, I recently found that a submitted manuscript had already been published by the same authors at a different journal. iThenticate reported a 98% similarity score. Not only did I reject the manuscript, but I alerted both my own publisher, and the editor of the journal that had already accepted the article. As EinC, I have also been contacted by an ethics review committee at a university investigating its own staff member for this kind of behaviour and requesting that I provide relevant information.

EinCs may also be invited to perform a variety of other tasks by virtue of their EinC position. For instance, I am regularly invited to be an external member of a promotion and/or tenure committee, and an invited speaker at conferences or seminars. I am also frequently invited to be an external examiner of PhD theses at universities globally. As far as my time allows, I always accept these invitations, and then undertake my responsibilities to the best of my ability. I feel that this is an important form of giving back to the community. I find that my role as EinC means that I am in demand because authors are genuinely interested in knowing how EinCs think about research topics, or methods problems, or other scholarly situations. Although I might be giving a talk about problematisation or context or theory, the questions that I am asked cross all possible domains of research: it is as if I am a mine of information to be tapped into, and my presence at the event provides that opportunity. Actually, I think that any senior academic should be well-positioned to answer these kinds of questions, and if I am not available then I try my best to find an alternate speaker who usually is not an EinC.

Once or twice a year, I organise an editorial board meeting, usually on the fringes of one of our major conferences, but sometimes virtually. All SEs and AEs are invited, and sometimes the editorial advisory board (EAB) members as well. There is a formal agenda of topics that are current and worthy of discussion. At these meetings, I present a publisher's report that includes data about submissions, time for review, acceptance levels, numbers of downloads, impact factor, and so on. I always invite SEs and AE to identify items for the agenda. There is also plenty of free time for discussion. It is important that the SEs and AEs get to meet each other, especially those who are newly appointed, since all their communications during the year are virtual unless they work in the same place or meet at other events.

Finally, I have regular communication with my editorial manager at the publisher's headquarters, the editorial assistants, and the production teams. These communications cover a wide range of topics and may occur as frequently as several times a day. For instance, there are communications regarding updates to the journal's website, decisions about which articles to include in the next issue, concerns about the review process, and policy issues that require publisher input. It is critical that the editor is in close contact with all the people who support the journal. I deal with the topic of editor-publisher interactions in more detail in Chap. 7.

All this communication takes a lot of time. EinCs really can't stint on the time: it takes as long as it takes, but an hour or 2 a day, 7 days a week, does not seem unreasonable. The EinC role might be considered a labour of love for this reason alone: it is not for the faint of heart or those who cannot commit time.

3

Cultural Values

Abstract This chapter focuses on the cultural values that the editor seeks to establish for the journal. These values may be informed by the members of the editorial advisory board, as well as senior and associate editors who work with the journal. The cultural values themselves evolve over time, and may change markedly when a new editor is appointed. Key values that I describe in this chapter include the duty of care that the journal/editor has for the journal's many stakeholders, the trust that we hope to create in the journal's institutions, the integrity that we need to incorporate in our daily practices, and the value of time since this is a precious resource for all stakeholders. I also provide a detailed discussion of the way diversity considerations are changing journal values, and explore how the journals and its many senior and associate editors may usefully be regarded as belonging to a family. Finally, I describe how the journal's culture can be communicated to its many stakeholders, the role of editorials penned by the editor, and the nature of the discretions and privileges that pertain to the editor, as well as their consequences.

For a journal to be successful, i.e. attract high-quality submissions, provide a high-quality review process, and publish high-quality articles that are downloaded, read, appreciated and cited by its intended audience, it is critical that a supporting infrastructure is in place. This infrastructure comprises not only such varied elements as an effective submission and review system, and policy guidelines for authors and reviewers, but most importantly the cultural values that inform how the journal operates and to which its many stakeholders are expected to subscribe. Examples of cultural values include the duty of care that the journal has for its many stakeholders, and the diversity that the journal subscribes to in terms of what kinds of research it seeks to publish and what are the characteristics of the editors who serve the journal. Although the cultural values may be seen to represent the position of the journal as a whole, and even its publisher, in practice they owe much to the personal vision of the EinC. Since EinCs are often contractually obliged to serve the journal and its many stakeholders, they also have a vested interest in the success of the journal. EinCs should have the opportunity to develop the set of cultural values that they believe is most conducive to the journal being successful. Creating, disseminating and enforcing these cultural values is thus a key responsibility for the editor, although other key internal stakeholders, such as the SE and AE as well as the members of the Editorial Advisory Board (EAB), may also participate. It is important to note that the culture and character of a journal can change over time, in particular when a new EinC is appointed. Such changes are, in my view healthy, which implies that it is not a good principle for an EinC to remain in the saddle for too long, as I explore in more detail below.

3.1 The Editorial Advisory Board

Some journals retain an EAB of scholars who, ostensibly, provide advice to the EinC and the journal more generally. The EAB often appears to comprise an assortment of 'the great and the good', a selection of senior, if not actually senile, scholars some of whom are in their twilight years and who are accorded respect in this way. Retired SEs may be 'promoted' to the EAB if they still wish to retain the association with the journal. When I write to the EAB I occasionally get a bounce and on checking find that the individual has passed away some months or years previously, but, embarrassingly, I didn't notice. The quicker of the EAB members may be willing to do the occasional review for the journal, often on an emergency basis where others have failed to deliver. A more passionate EinC may be able to energise the EAB into taking more substantive actions on behalf of the journal, such as promoting it at the events that they attend, or encouraging submissions by their colleagues. I do from time to time reach out to individual EAB members to solicit their feedback on journal developments, for instance regarding new policies, changes to submission guidelines, special issues, and controversial topics that are the subject of editorials. Their inputs here are invaluable and it is fair to say that several have provided commentary on earlier drafts of the current book. Removing people from the EAB, other than through their passing, is not easy and they seldom resign of their own accord. I recall how a long-retired professor, who had ceased to do any research for at least two decades, nevertheless stubbornly refused the 'invitation' to step down, even though he could not make any useful contribution to the journal. His passing a year later 'resolved' the situation, but as EinC I felt strangely powerless to take any humble action other than to let time take its toll in its own time. For this reason, the appointment of a new EinC may provide the only easy opportunity to refresh the EAB.

3.2 The Evolution of Cultural Values

A journal's cultural values are likely to evolve over an extended period of time. An EinC with a short tenure may find it hard to effect significant or long-lasting change, the more so as his/her successor may want to align the journal with a completely different set of values. Some EinCs have tenures as short as 3 years, which seems a pitifully short duration to even try to achieve much. Personally, I'd argue for at least a five-year minimum, with the option of extending it to ten if the publisher and other key stakeholders are satisfied with the EinC's performance. At the same time, if an EinC is in harness for too long, and I am aware of journals where the EinC has not changed in over 30 years, then there is significant risk that too much power is concentrated in the hands of too few people. The corollary of this is that many other talented people will not be appointed as EinCs. As a result, the field in which the journal exists will be impoverished by the absence of a greater diversity of perspectives that might have otherwise been enabled.

A newly appointed EinC is unlikely to be able to effect significant cultural change in the short-term (unless the EinC appoints a whole new cohort of SEs and AEs) as it would be too disruptive to existing norms, confusing to both authors and readers, and potentially too divisive among the existing SEs and AEs. However, in the longer term such change is very plausible. For instance, I can fully appreciate that a newly appointed EinC may be uncomfortable with some of the current SEs and AEs if their views regarding research or review processes differ too much from the EinC's own views. However, these people are often appointed on a multi-year basis and would normally expect to serve out their terms, which may be as long as 5 years. Thus, the EinC must devise and enact cultural change with care. For instance, new SEs and AEs can be brought on board and may be assigned the lion's share of newly submitted manuscripts, while the longer-standing SEs and AEs may find that they are assigned fewer manuscripts to handle than used to be the case, or even none at all. This shift might be sufficient to persuade them to step down voluntarily. However, there are risks here. An EinC with a long tenure ahead may, hopefully inadvertently, damage the journal by bending its culture and values too far towards his/her own vision of what a journal in that discipline should look like, or what kind of research is publishable. This may lead to an overly narrow scope of the kinds of articles that the journal publishes.

The actual cultural values that can be ascribed to journals are multifaceted. For instance, they may include: what kinds of research articles the EinC believes the journal should (or should not) publish; what kind of review process the journal should provide to submitting authors; what should be the characteristics of the SEs and AEs as well as reviewers. The principle of diversity could apply to all the above issues: as EinC I wish to see a diversity of submissions from a diversity of authors handled by a diversity of editorial team members. This diversity extends from topics to methods to epistemologies. I hope that these various stakeholders will be of different genders, ethnicities, intellectual persuasions, born, trained or currently working in a diversity of countries. There are also cultural attributes that govern the relations between the editorial team: personally, I think that in our communications with each other we should be direct, friendly, polite, honest, yet where necessary robust.

My own view is that any EinC should make it very clear what kinds of research is sought and appreciated, and what is not. All EinCs are likely to have some sense of what they are (or are not) looking for. At the same time, EinCs need to be aware of the natural diversity of the field of research that the journal they edit seeks to publish, and hence avoid excluding too many topics or methods on the grounds that they don't fit the EinC's vision. For instance, novelty is often highly rated, whether of theoretical or methodological contribution, analytical technique or even topic. Some journals publish replication studies, systematic literature reviews and agendas that lack an empirical basis, but many do not. I have a strong expectation that authors will contribute to both theory and practice, i.e. make a contribution that is valuable both for other researchers and for practitioners. I personally favour both engaged scholarship, where academic researchers and industry practitioners collaborate on projects that are practice-centric, and indigenous research, where the research design is situated in and draws on a local context for its concepts. With regard to the former, I encourage the undertaking of what we call 'practitioner research', where we do not expect to see a contribution to theory (as is normally the case in academic research) but instead expect to see prescriptive guidelines and advice for practice. Concerning the latter, I encourage indigenous theorising, where the local context informs the theory that is developed to explain behaviour in that context. My views on context are explored in some detail in Davison and Martinsons (2016). I also have a strong interest in publishing research that addresses the concerns of non-managerial practitioner stakeholders, as well as citizens, consumers, natural ecosystems and the environment. My interest does not mandate that these stakeholders benefit from the research that we publish or that theory be indigenous, nor do I exclude manuscripts that make other contributions, but I am particularly happy to see research that is oriented towards non-managerial stakeholders in practice or that theorises indigenously and I would like the journals that I edit to be known to be receptive to this kind of work.

3.3 The Duty of Care for the Journal's Stakeholders

While the identification of the topics that the editor believes are in scope for publication is very much discipline specific, there are other issues that are more generic. For instance, at the journals I edit, we adhere to a strong principle of care for different stakeholders (Davison and Tarafdar 2022). We identify these stakeholders as: authors, SEs, AEs, reviewers, readers, and the discipline in which the journal is situated. Our care for authors is reflected in our intention to provide them with constructive and insightful feedback within a reasonable time frame. With respect to time, I note that editors, reviewers and authors all have a tendency to miss their deadlines. Reviewers are late and need to be encouraged to complete their reviews. Authors miss deadlines and then find that the MMS locks them out, so an extension to the deadline is needed. Meanwhile, both SEs and AEs are often late, whether in assigning reviewers or writing reports. In order to keep abreast of these issues, which change continually, I make a point of logging in to the MMS on a daily basis, 7 days a week, 365 days a year. I can miss a day or two, but I try not to. Although the MMS will send auto-reminders, I find that personal reminders from myself are more effective, as I can tailor them to the individual and try to adopt a more friendly tone, since MMS messages tend to be abrupt.

To give an idea of the extent of these communications, below I provide a list of manuscript management situations that I can see on the MMS for one of the journals I edit. Each of these situations has a number (zero or more) that indicates how many manuscripts are in this situation. For all non-zero situations, there is a link that I can click to see the details of all the manuscripts in that situation, including all metadata, details of reviewers, SEs and AEs, authors, etc. In the case of delays, I can see which author, reviewer, AE or SE is delayed and by how many days. There are also links to send emails (through the MMS) to any of these stakeholders, as well as the EA, for each manuscript. The list of situations below has been customised to meet my requirements, i.e. when I took over as EinC many of these situations were not indicated and I had to request the MMS technical support team that they be included. When I look at this list, I can quickly see roughly where there are problems or bottlenecks, and by clicking on the various links I can find out exactly what the problem is and can then contact people to take the necessary action. Elsewhere in the MMS, there are search and report systems where I can search the MMS for specific issues, e.g. the details of manuscripts written by authors in a particular country, or the details of which manuscripts are handled by a specific SE or AE, the acceptance rate for research articles, or the number of times articles have been downloaded, etc.

- Manuscripts waiting to be assigned by me to an SE.
- Manuscripts waiting to be assigned by the SE to an AE.
- Manuscripts waiting for the AE to select reviewers.
- Manuscripts where the reviewers have been selected but not yet invited.
- Manuscripts where the reviewers have been invited, but the reviewers have not yet accepted the invitation.
- Manuscripts waiting for reviewers to complete their evaluations.
- Manuscripts where the reviewers are late in completing their evaluations.
- Manuscripts where the review has been rescinded by the AE.
- Manuscripts waiting for the AE to make a recommendation.
- Manuscripts where the AE recommendation is overdue.
- Manuscripts waiting for the SE to make a recommendation.
- Manuscripts where the SE recommendation is overdue.
- Manuscripts waiting for the EinC to make a decision.
- Original manuscripts under consideration.
- Revised manuscripts under consideration.
- Manuscripts waiting for authors to revise them following review.
- Manuscripts where the authors have missed the deadline to revise.
- Manuscripts unsubmitted by the EA because of submission errors.
- Accepted manuscripts that are queued for production.

We also aim to help the authors through a constructive review process so that they can improve their manuscript to the point where it can be accepted for publication. In all our communications, we aim to be polite and friendly, no matter the circumstances. Our care for readers means that we want to publish articles that are high quality, that will inspire and challenge them to think about research topics in a new way. Meanwhile, we must also demonstrate care for SEs and AEs, as well as reviewers. These people need clear guidelines for the standards that we expect of them, and sufficient time to complete quality reviews. We are careful not to overload SEs or AEs with too many manuscripts to handle at one time, and indeed allow them to take 'sabbaticals' from the handling of new manuscripts if they request it. For instance, a long-serving SE recently requested that she be assigned no new manuscripts for seven months as she needed to devote time to family matters.

Where the discipline is concerned, caring for the discipline implies not only that we try to advance the discipline by publishing articles that advance our knowledge, but also that we not publish articles that are arguably out of scope and so may dilute the discipline (Davison and Tarafdar 2022). This is tricky, since the question of what is in or out of scope for any discipline is quite subjective particularly when one is researching at the edges of the discipline, or engaging in cross- or multi-disciplinary work, where contributions are being made in multiple disciplines (Tarafdar and Davison 2018). Nevertheless, we do encounter manuscripts that are demonstrably out of scope. These often involve research designs that are situated in an online context, yet where the problem is primarily central to another discipline, e.g. Marketing, Economics, Law, and the contributions that the authors make in the manuscript are directed to the audience in that other discipline. The Information Systems aspects of the manuscript are limited to the context, and thus the discipline scarcely benefits from the research. This does not mean that the research is badly done, but simply that it does not fit the journal.

3.4 Trust

A second cultural dimension is trust. We develop and maintain trust with the stakeholders mentioned above. We hope that authors will entrust their manuscripts to us, knowing that the review process is fair but thorough, and will be completed in reasonable time. We similarly trust that reviewers will be impartial and honest in their critique, taking the care and trouble to engage in a trenchant analysis of what the manuscript offers. Rarely, we may need to return a review to a reviewer if we feel that the quality expectation has not been met. Equally we may return a manuscript to an author if we feel that the author has not sufficiently revised the manuscript following review. As EinC, I place a significant amount of trust in SEs and AEs who support the journal. I trust in their professionalism, their generosity of time and energy, their selection of appropriately qualified reviewers.

3.5 Integrity

A third and related cultural dimension is integrity. This is central to our work. We expect that all members of the review team will act according to the highest standards of integrity when they are charged with handling the review of a manuscript. Although reviewers do not know the identity of authors, editors must know, both so as to avoid asking authors to review their own manuscript and to avoid potential conflicts of interest such as inviting the authors' colleagues as reviewers. Academic disciplines are often close-knit, with many interwoven relationships. As a result, I commonly find myself in the position of knowing the people who submit their manuscripts to the journal; indeed, they may even be my co-authors, students or colleagues. I cannot deny them the right to submit their manuscripts to the journal for this reason, but where necessary I can recuse myself from handling their manuscripts. I have created a mechanism whereby a former ME of the journal takes my role as EinC for these manuscripts. This mechanism also allows me to be the (co)author of a manuscript submitted to the same journal, a practice that the publisher explicitly endorses. However, it is important to note that some journals explicitly prohibit the EinC from being listed as the author of a manuscript during the course of the EinC's tenure. Nevertheless, it is not surprising that EinCs would want to submit to the journals they edit. To some extent, the EinC's appointment is made on the basis of the commonality of interest between the editor and the journal. For these manuscripts, the MMS blocks my access to information, so I cannot see who are the SE, AE and reviewers. What is critical here is that we always adhere to the most rigorous standards of professional integrity. Manuscripts should be assessed on the basis of merit alone. There cannot be any personal considerations.

3.6 The Value of Time

Timeliness is an issue that crops up regularly. Authors expect that their manuscripts will be reviewed promptly. Our indicative expectation is that we will complete reviews for a submitted manuscript within 90 days. This time covers all the activities indicated in Fig. 2.1, i.e. initial screening, initial review by the SE and AE, selection of and communication with reviewers, reviewing, report writing by the SE and AE, and finally decision reaching and communicating by the EinC. On average we do make this 90-day deadline, but authors frequently expect a much shorter time frame and may even ask when their manuscript will be accepted (!) just a week after initial submission. In reality reviewers often need more time than we allow (6 weeks) and indeed authors also need more time to revise their manuscripts than we suggest (1–3 months depending on the nature of the revisions). All these extensions conspire to delay the review process, often considerably and so sometimes a year may be needed for one round of a review and revision process. When multiple rounds of review-revision are needed before a final decision (accept or reject) can be made, multiple years may also be required. Therefore, we regard keeping to deadlines as a matter of respect to all parties. Reviewers who hope to be invited to join the journal as AEs should bear in mind that delayed submission of reviews will not impress us as to their suitability. I always check reviewer records for this kind of information before offering an AE position. From a knowledge dissemination perspective, these extended delays are not at all ideal. The lapse of several years from problem formulation to data collection, manuscript writing, reviewing and (finally) publication is not at all conducive to scholarly progress.

3.7 The Hazards and Delights of Diversity

Where diversity is concerned, I strive to avoid political correctness and instead to achieve a fair balance. I see no benefit in appointing unqualified people as AEs solely so as to ensure that diversity criteria are met. But I do see benefits in trying to ensure that the SEs and AEs are as diverse in character as is reasonably possible. For instance, at one of the two journals I edit, we have a male-to-female gender ratio of approximately 2:1, which is similar to the distribution of researchers in the discipline that these two journals belong to. Around half of the SEs and AEs are of European/Caucasian descent, a third are Chinese, a tenth Indian. Only 3% are of African origin, which seems disproportionately low, but unfortunately the proportion of people of African origin in this discipline is even lower at 2%. As EinC, I want all authors to feel welcome. If we are seen to have SEs and AEs from different genders and cultural backgrounds, who are experts in the application of different methods, and who themselves publish in the same journal, then the implicit message to prospective authors is that we welcome a diversity of research from a diversity of people. Diversity of topic is also important for a journal that positions itself as a publication outlet for a range of ideas, both orthodox and iconoclastic. But this diversity may be hard to perceive unless it is clearly presented, so at each of the journals that I edit, I recently published editorials that laid out in considerable detail the evidence of this diversity (Davison 2021a, b). These editorials are free to download and are also prominently linked on the home page of the journal. I anticipate updating the information on the webpage as it changes. In short, diversity matters but it is not enough to be diverse (on multiple criteria): we must also be seen to be diverse by all our stakeholders, and for that diversity to be a spur to further action.

3.8 A Journal Is a Family

When I introduce new AEs to the journal, and particularly at our regular editorial board meetings, I make a point of welcoming them to the 'family' of the journal. For some, this is a curious metaphor to use, but my intention is that we should work together in concert and support each other like the members of an extended family. This does not in any way prevent each individual from having their own unique perspective on research, nor does it require them to agree with each other on research matters, but it does imply that we have a common set of values that reflect why we are associated with the journal, what kind of review and publication processes we champion, how we relate to each other. For instance, I encourage SEs and AEs to engage in a conversation about a manuscript that has been assigned to them. They can together work out if the manuscript is strong enough to be sent for review or if it should be desk rejected. They can also jointly consider who would be the most suitable reviewers. For instance, they might identify one reviewer each, and pick a third from those nominated by the author(s). Although SEs and AEs have different roles to play, there is much advantage to be gained from a collaborative approach to the review management process, especially where the identification of reviewers is concerned. If they share a similar set of values, it is that much easier for them to engage in a conversation and reach consensus about the process, even if each sees the merits or faults of the manuscript differently. I would like to take the metaphor of the family further and suggest that we should include the authors who submit manuscripts to the journals as members of the extended family as well. We work with these authors to help them along the path towards publication. We hope that they will review manuscripts for the same journal and 1 day we may welcome them as new AEs. Ultimately, it takes a family to get a manuscript published.

3.9 Communicating the Culture

EinCs can communicate the cultural values of the journal through a number of different channels. Different stakeholder groups are the targets of these communications. For instance, the journal's website potentially provides a good location for a repository of documents, such as policies and guidelines, which are of particular salience to prospective authors, but also reviewers. While guidelines for authors and reviewers will not change very often, the EinC does need to be able to update these documents whenever needed. Such updates might be effected directly, but it is more likely that the EinC will need to send the update to a publishing contact who is responsible for website maintenance. In my experience, these updates are painless and simple, but I am aware of other journals (notably those published by a university press) where it can take many months for updates to be effected, because of a lack of commitment of resources to this task by the publisher.

All authors are recommended to familiarise themselves with current journal policies and perspectives as they craft their manuscripts and certainly before submission. This is not just a matter of formatting standards, but rather of ensuring that there is a good fit between the manuscript being submitted and the journal. Too many manuscripts are rejected without review due to a lack of fit that could have been detected and corrected had the authors troubled to check out the relevant information on the website. The EinC may also communicate with key stakeholders, notably SEs and AEs, via email or social media channels, though I personally tend to shun the latter. It is important that these people are aware of current cultural perspectives at the journal, for they are on the front line of assessing manuscripts and need to provide feedback that is consistent with those perspectives.

I try to organise an editorial board meeting either in person (usually on the fringes of a conference) or virtually, once or twice a year, so as to provide the opportunity for SEs and AEs to meet each other, ask me questions, and learn about the development of the journal. The publisher's representative often attends to deliver a presentation from the publisher's perspective. Editorial board meetings do not need to be too formal, but they are invaluable as a way of getting to know the other members of the board.

3.10 Editorials and Opinions

Apart from website updates, the EinC can also write editorials for publication in the journal, in which messages for the journal's readership are communicated. Not all EinCs write such editorials, and for some it might be a chore, but I feel that the genre of an editorial opinion piece provides an excellent opportunity for the EinC to reach out to readers, authors and other stakeholders on a regular basis about important issues. Prospective authors in particular may benefit from editorial opinions, since these opinions provide a unique insight into the thinking of the EinC about the journal itself. I always alert the SEs and AEs of the journal to new editorials because they too need to be familiar with the emerging policies of the journal and may find that their task of writing up a report is easier when they can refer to an editorial to justify a particular point. Although editorials are rarely cited, they are often read by the wider audience of the journal. Much like a regular newspaper column, they may be eagerly awaited. The personal feedback that I get, often from people whom I do not know, that they enjoyed reading the editorials is much appreciated.

During my tenure as EinC, I have written well over 40 editorials, all of which can be downloaded for free from the respective journals' websites.[1] Other than accepting articles for publication, writing editorials is one of my most enjoyable tasks as EinC. I find inspiration for editorials in a wide range of sources, from general science to literature to politics, as well as in the nitty-gritty details of how journals are edited. My editorials cover a very wide range of topics that are relevant both to the specific audiences of the journals I edit but also more broadly. While many are written by myself alone, others I have written in collaboration with one or more of my SE colleagues, as well as occasionally with other scholars. I provide a complete index of these editorials in Appendix B, but I summarise a few that are particularly related to a journal's cultural values in the following paragraphs. I suggest that the topics covered in these editorials are relevant for all EinCs in the humanities and social sciences in particular, and that EinCs will do well to consider if they need to modify any of their current procedures.

I start off with *cultural bias in reviews* (Davison 2014). This is an important topic because all of us are biased, whether we are aware of it or not, and our biases are particularly visible when we write our opinions, which is something that reviewers do. While reviewing a submission to a journal involves documenting one's analysis of the manuscript, that analysis is likely to be informed

---

[1] https://onlinelibrary.wiley.com/page/journal/13652575/homepage/editorials.htm

by one's biases. A common bias involves a preference (perhaps unconscious) for what I term 'mainstream' thinking, or the expectation that research should fit snugly into the current orthodoxy of the discipline, such that it can usefully inform the majority of researchers. When research falls outside this orthodox perspective (and each reviewer will decide individually what is orthodox or not), then biases can emerge. Some reviewers are open to new ideas, but many are suspicious. For instance, we encourage authors to develop new theory, but reviewers often query the need for new theory and seem reluctant to allow that a new theory is called for. This is problematic, in my view. Advances in knowledge are not limited to what is consistent with orthodox thinking, and a persistent advocacy of mainstream topics, methods, theory and epistemology seems to constitute a form of discrimination, especially if that orthodoxy is associated with particular ethnic groups or research subcultures. This kind of cultural bias functions in an exclusive fashion, seeking to impose a cultural hegemony on what kind of research is legitimate, and what is not. I often find myself in the position of rejecting a submission because it has failed to take significant steps in a novel direction, or to challenge the orthodoxy. For instance, scholars in developing countries are very fond of taking a well-established theory or model from the (predominantly Western) literature and testing it with local data. This kind of research is safe but not very interesting. It does not lead to new insights about what is significant in the local context. It does not tell us about the local or indigenous cultural concepts that significantly influence behaviour in the local context. As a result, we can't learn anything new. All we find out is that the well-established theory also works well in this new context. My intention in this editorial was to sensitise readers to the existence of cultural bias in reviews, and then to reflect on how they could combat this bias when they are in the position of reviewing others' work.

Most authors acknowledge the imperfections of their work and thus include a 'limitations' section towards the end of their articles. However, *limitations themselves have limitations* (Davison 2017a)! For instance, many authors take a template approach to the limitations of their research in multiple journals and disciplines. The text of the limitations sections barely varies across multiple articles by different authors, and the limitations section seems to function as no more than a repository for all the things that authors never actually planned to do in the first place, or even for things that they did do that weren't very well justified or successful. For instance, researchers who used a cross-sectional survey design might admonish themselves for this poor methodological choice and counsel future researchers to use a longitudinal research design, yet hardly any researchers ever do so: the cross-sectional design persists. Other researchers bemoan their failure to study a broader population (they only studied a narrowly defined population) or to employ a more rigorous research method. These kinds of limitations seem highly disingenuous: the selection of a population is surely deliberate, so to call your own research limiting seems to be akin to requesting rejection; meanwhile, to argue that some methods are more rigorous than others suggests a woefully inadequate appreciation of what rigour actually means, viz.: the correct application of methods in a given context. I urge authors to reflect more honestly on the real limitations of their research, rather than indulging in feeble self-flagellation, while reviewers need to critique the limitations as much as they critique the rest of the manuscript.

Shifting baselines are a perennial issue in research: with the passing of time, what used to be familiar and contemporary slips into history (Davison and Tarafdar 2018). More insidiously, what used to be considered of critical importance may also slip away. In this editorial we commented on the prevailing fashion for research to be driven by (inter alia) atheoretical designs and for that research to make little in the way of a novel theoretical contribution. Historically, researchers in this discipline were expected to organise their research designs around a strong theoretical anchor, but a growing number of contemporary scholars appear to take a rather cavalier attitude to theory, regarding it as optional at best. This thus constitutes a shifting baseline. In different disciplines, it may be that different baselines shift, yet the impact may be the same: an existential threat to the discipline. Journals, and their editors, are often seen as custodians of both history and present practice: EinCs in particular serve as gatekeepers to what is or is not published. An EinC certainly has the prerogative to desk reject a submission that fails to meet the basic criteria for publication. But that prerogative comes with a huge responsibility: authors on the leading edge of the discipline, those seeking to shift the baseline for instance, may charge the editor with over-zealous protection of the past or over-cautious restraint on development of the field. Editors must thus balance between an appropriate regard for novelty, an openness to what may seem to them like alien thinking, an appreciation of iconoclastic research that opens up new frontiers, a respect for the past and its long-established standards, and a sense of their own role as both custodians of tradition and champions of advances in knowledge. EinCs may be faulted no matter what position they take, whether by the conservative traditionalists or the liberal Machiavellians. They have to be particularly careful to avoid the situation where a journal is hijacked by a particular interest group with an agenda to shift the baseline in a particular direction. Shifting baselines can be a symptom of progress, though they can also be a symptom of a deeper malaise in society and as such need to be treated with caution. Editors have the responsibility to manage the baselines with care.

An iconoclast is defined as 'someone who does something that others say can't be done' (Berns 2010). Is there room for *iconoclasm in research* (Davison 2020b)? I suggest that iconoclastic thinking is a valuable part of research design and urge authors to try and think more iconoclastically, i.e. not just to accept the normative and incremental research design and contribution process. In an era of rapid change, notably in technology, more radical research designs that move faster than the more customary incrementalism may be called for. Artificial Intelligence is one domain where more rapid advances in knowledge could be anticipated. Neuroscience could be another. Researchers are still standing on the shoulders of giants, their intellectual forebears, but they are advocating more radical steps ahead. But iconoclasm is not for the faint of heart! It entails considerable risk, especially if your ideas are rejected or disproven: public ridicule might be the least of the consequences. It requires a certain disdain for the adulation of others, a willingness to go alone and challenge the status quo. Nevertheless, an academic journal is a reasonably safe stage to work on: the audience is necessarily limited in scope, and the fundamental idea of academic freedom acts as a strong shield against attack.

All research articles include references, yet how authors select references sometimes seems quite mysterious. As a result, we found good reason to make recommendations about what we called '*The Art of Referencing*' (Tarafdar and Davison 2020). We started by noting the egregious behaviour of editors (at all levels) who essentially compel authors to cite their own (the editors') articles as a condition of the research being accepted. This behaviour is beyond the pale: coercive referencing is abhorrent. However, voluntarily citing research that is published in the journal that you are submitting to might be seen as a form of respect, and is certainly a way of connecting to the ongoing intellectual conversation that takes place in the pages of the journal. Beyond coercion, some authors tend to overcite (perhaps indulging in name dropping), a few under cite and a few self-cite to a preposterous extent, essentially rendering a blind review process impossible. My rule of thumb for a regular research article is that no more than 10% of the length should be taken up by references. In a review article it may be more, perhaps 15%. These are not magic numbers and it is more important that relevant material be cited and referenced. But 'gobs' of a dozen or more references to support a single point seem rather ridiculous: two or three should suffice. If the 12 are essential, could they be spaced out over a few sentences? Could we see what is the exact point of citing each reference? Cites to articles in obscure locations (such as behind corporate firewalls) that are essentially unfindable need to be avoided, since readers and reviewers should be able to access any material that is cited. Cites to articles written in languages other than the language of the article itself are also awkward: the authors should not assume that the readers will be polyglottally familiar with other languages. The editorial goes into much more depth than presented here, but we do urge authors to be careful with their referencing. Referencing is a way of demonstrating appreciation for those on whose shoulders we stand and saying 'thank you'.

The last editorial that I discuss here concerns the idea that research and researchers should be *responsible* both to their research community and to a broader set of stakeholders. The Responsible Research for Business and Management Alliance (RRBM)[2] is one of the champions of these efforts and in 2019 we issued a call for manuscripts, in conjunction with RRBM, for a special issue devoted to responsible research (Davison et al. 2023a). Our view is that we, as editors but also as researchers, have moral obligation to make the world a better place. This may seem like a tall order, but it is not a new one: several authors (e.g. Walsham 2012) have commented on the need for researchers to take up the moral cudgel on behalf of our planet more robustly. Each researcher will interpret 'responsible' in different ways. Our take was that research needs to contribute not only to economic, but also to social, personal and environmental contexts (see Clarke and Davison 2020 for a critical take on researcher perspectives). Responsible research is not (necessarily) the same as green research: Elliot and Webster (2017) point out that too much so-called green research takes the view that green can help the corporate bottom line, yet fails to identify net benefits for the environment. Sustainability is a prominent theme in responsible research, tapping into contemporary discourse regarding such issues as climate change, pollution, and all the human-induced impact on the environment that is often referred to as the Anthropocene. In championing responsible research, we encourage researchers to examine their own motives as researchers: whom do they wish to serve? Who are the beneficiaries of their research? How can they contribute to making the world a better place?

3.11 Editorial Discretions, Privileges and Consequences

EinCs have considerable discretion to orient the journals that they edit in particular directions, catering to different audiences. The cultural values of the journal, which to a large extent reflect the personality and values of the EinC, are certainly one manifestation of that discretion. The special issues that the

---

[2] http://rrbm.network

EinC approves, or commissions, are another. In each of these situations, the EinC has an opportunity to take a stand, to champion a particular set of objectives, to facilitate research on a particular genre or topic and to empower some researchers to take advantage of these various opportunities. There are many good things that an EinC can enable, but is there also a dark side? Any of the choices that I have described in this chapter could have a darker side, a different way of looking at things that might confer an advantage on a different set of researchers. For instance, the vast majority of special issue proposals are rejected, but those reject decisions could be queried. Researchers who do not feel the obligation to make the world a better place, but instead only look to their own selfish interests, might be distressed by the Responsible Research special issue that I describe above. They might even decide to boycott the journal in the future, refusing not only to submit manuscripts to it, but also to refrain from citing articles published in it and to refuse to review submissions to it.

In taking a position, the EinC is, to a significant degree, placing him/herself in a vulnerable position, a hostage to fortune. If a significant proportion of the previously loyal supporters of the journal are sufficiently annoyed by the EinC's actions and decide to find greener pastures elsewhere, then the journal may experience an existential problem: a lack of viable submissions. Where does the EinC draw the line or decide how far beyond the comfort zone of the current supporters it is safe to go? In a niche journal this is a very real problem and EinCs need to tread very warily indeed. They will be well advised to seek the countenance of their EABs and SEs/AEs. In broader journals with a larger base of stakeholders, the magnitude of the risk may be smaller yet is not insignificant. I recall a recent situation where a premier journal was essentially hijacked by a subset of its regular contributors, AEs and SEs, led by the EinC, who arranged for a major change of focus that ostracised many potential contributing authors, myself included. The articles that were published under this new regime were so different to past practice, and indeed so disconnected with the field, that many authors felt that the number of premier journals to which they could aspire to submit their work had significantly diminished. The situation remained in this hiatus for 5 years until a new editor, with a broader agenda, was appointed, and many in the community heaved a sigh of relief.

4

Sourcing Content and Authors

Abstract This chapter deals with the important topic of content, i.e. the research papers that the editor aims to accept for publication in the journal. I differentiate between newly and long-established journals, explore how content can be commissioned or sourced from different venues, and also explain the unique value proposition of special issues. Quality is a key criterion for sourcing to which the editor must pay special attention, since poor quality publications will damage the journal's reputation. Finally, I consider the motivations of authors to submit their research to a journal.

If a journal is popular or occupies a significant niche, it may be blessed with a huge number of (hopefully high-quality) submissions. From such a largesse of material, assuming that you have a large enough number of dedicated SEs and AEs, you will not be too hard-pressed to work with the authors to deliver sufficient high-quality finished articles to satisfy your publication manager. Newly established and less popular journals, on the other hand, may lack this supply chain of suitable material. The EinC then has to consider very carefully how to source appropriate content. In effect, this means that the EinC has to persuade aspiring authors to submit manuscripts (of various types) in which novel contributions to knowledge are made. Exactly what is 'appropriate' may vary widely: some journals are happy to publish replications of prior work, others insist on novelty. Many journals demand strong theoretical contributions, yet others may prefer to see strong contributions to practice. Some journal editors are open to new, alien or iconoclastic ideas whereas others prefer less intellectually challenging topics that will be appreciated by a wide audience. As a research discipline evolves, so the topics, methods, theories and data may shift. Journal editors need to decide how the journal should position itself regarding these shifts: does it take the Machiavellian stance of favouring the new, insurgent research that iconoclastically breaks with the past, in the hope that it will be publishing the new trends, or does it try to stymie the pace of innovation by keeping to the already familiar topics and standards? Howsoever these questions are answered, each EinC needs to position the journal in a way that ensures its continued relevance for its audience, even as that audience evolves.

The actions that an EinC takes may vary according to the status of the journal. If the journal is newly established, then the EinC's first task is to build up a competent roster of SEs and perhaps AEs, as well as an EAB that can provide constructive advice. The EinC can try to commission content, i.e. to invite prominent scholars personally to submit a manuscript. However, it might be that several weeks or months pass before the first invited submissions arrive, and a year or more before any of those submissions make it through the review process to a point where they are ready for publication. In the first few years, especially if the topic area of the journal is narrow, the EinC may struggle to attract sufficient numbers of manuscripts away from other, more established venues.

4.1 Content and Newly Established Journals

For instance, in 1997, a newly established journal folded after just 1 year (four issues) of publication. This journal was named '*The Journal of Failures and Lessons Learned in IT Management*' (*JFLLITM*). The niche was a reasonable one, with no other journal focusing on IT failures. However, it is not always easy to get access to cases of failures involving IT management and not all researchers appreciate the value of such studies of failures. The EinC of *JFLLITM* was an established and respected scholar, but it appears that the journal was not able to attract sufficient volume of high-quality submissions to survive. Some of the articles that were published in that single first year may have been invited by the editor, and the colleagues of the editor may have been more than happy to help out, but a journal has to stand on its own feet, i.e. without the support of friends who respond to an invitation to submit, if it is to thrive in the long-term.

In contrast, in 1999 I and a colleague founded a journal that I still edit: the *'Electronic Journal of Information Systems in Developing Countries'* (*EJISDC*). At the time we recognised that there were a couple of other journals in this niche, but that the demand for a journal on IS in Developing Countries was high. We were also critical of the editorial line taken by the other journals and believed that we could compete effectively. Our first issue appeared a year after establishment, with 25 articles published in the first year and an acceptance rate of 25%, which is admittedly high for an academic journal. Only two manuscripts were invited in the first year, and thus we made the decision to promote the journal very widely so as to attract submissions. Today 24 years later, the *EJISDC* thrives and we publish 36–48 articles a year, with an acceptance rate closer to 12%.

4.2 Commissioning Content

As noted above, EinCs can commission content by inviting selected individuals, for instance EAB members or other prominent scholars, to write an opinion piece for the journal. Given the nature of an opinion, these manuscripts tend to be reviewed a little less rigorously than is the case for research articles. Our primary objective in reviewing an opinion manuscript is to enhance its consumability by the audience. This may require some honing of the opinion itself, for instance so as to make it more clear or focused. It may also involve rendering the opinion in a way that it is comprehensible to a wide range of readers. For instance, opinions are, necessarily, personal, and thus often reflect personal circumstances or cultural contexts that may not be familiar to some readers. I suggest that commissioned articles should be the exception not the rule. It might be that a whole issue of commissioned opinion articles could be published if there is a contemporary situation that warrants such attention, for example a major anniversary, but more usually these commissioned manuscripts are published occasionally and on an exceptional basis. Publishing too many will have the effect of diluting the journal's integrity, since it may seem that if you are a member of 'the club', by virtue of your age, experience, senility, gender, race, or just personal connection with the EinC, then you get a 'free pass' to publish in the journal. Junior scholars in particular may harbour such suspicions, yet they are the people that the EinC least wants to form a negative impression given that they are the authors who have the most to contribute in the future.

4.3 Sourcing Content from Conferences

Prospective authors may find the journal through search engine optimisation techniques or via the journal's website. They can also be contacted at conferences, via personal networks and through word of mouth. We regularly organise 'manuscript development workshops' where we invite authors to submit ideas for discussion in a workshop setting, with a view to giving them feedback that will help them develop their ideas into fully fledged submissions. Editors who attend conferences might consider approaching authors of particularly good papers to encourage them to submit to a specific journal, or could hand out leaflets for the journal, or could even sponsor the conference in some way so as to gain extra visibility. If the conference is thematically organised, then a special issue of the journal could be organised out of the conference theme, though it will be important to ensure that quality standards are upheld.

For instance, as the EinC of a journal (*EJISDC*) that focuses on research in developing countries, I arranged for the publisher to offer €500 of prize money to best papers at a conference held in Yaoundé, Cameroon. I personally attended the conference, worked with the conference organisers to identify prize winners, and then participated in the prize awards ceremony. I also arranged for the authors to submit their manuscripts to the journal, though not to a special issue, and I must emphasise that this was not a matter of automatic acceptance. All these manuscripts were subject to the usual rigorous review process and ultimately only two were accepted for publication. However, both the publisher and the journal received welcome publicity, for relatively little cost, in an under-represented market. The prize winners were also happy, since even a fraction of €500 was a significant and unexpected appreciation of their work, while the authors of the two papers accepted for publication in the journal received additional kudos for their work.

4.4 Sourcing via Special Issues

Special issues can provide a valuable way of focusing on new topics, and indeed constitute a significant part of the business model of many journals. I am aware of journals that appear to publish a hundred or more special issues annually. This is an astonishing number, and I cannot but imagine that the quality control process regarding how these special issues are approved is very weak. Indeed, I have personally been invited by some publishers if I would like to edit a special issue on a topic of my choice, for publication in a journal that appears to be disciplinary specific, except that I don't work in that discipline, so how this invitation adds up to anything sensible I don't know. I am certain that editing such a special issue will not do my reputation any good at all.

Given this kind of concern, and the likelihood that less scrupulous researchers may imagine that a special issue offers them opportunity to publish their own work and that of their friends with minimal oversight, the EinC has to be extraordinarily careful when vetting special issue proposals. In my experience the vast majority are utterly unsuitable, at least for the journals that I edit, and as a result I accept only 1–2% of the proposals submitted. I expect that the guest editors of special issues will work hard to find sufficient high-quality manuscripts that meet the expectations of the journal. At the two journals I edit, we have organised special issues on a variety of different topics over the last 15 years with varying degrees of success[1,2] We encourage interested authors to send an extended abstract (and a hundred or more may do so), in order to get initial feedback that will help them craft their final submission, though this feedback can also be a way to filter out submissions that are unsuitable without going through a full review process. The more popular special issues may ultimately receive as many as 60 or more submissions, with perhaps 6–8 surviving the review process, i.e. an accept rate that approaches 10–15%. More commonly, and in particular if the special issue topic occupies a small niche, 20–30 submissions are received and no more than four are accepted. On rare occasions, very small numbers of manuscripts are submitted (often because the guest editors failed to promote it effectively) and in some cases no manuscripts are accepted at all: all are rejected during the review process.

The acceptance rates for special issues are often somewhat higher than the rate for regular research articles, and so special issues can be seen as offering a somewhat easier route to publication. This does not mean that a quality review process is absent or that the manuscripts themselves are of a lower quality, but rather it reflects how special issues work: while they target a narrow area of focus, they also bring to bear the resources of topic experts who are well-positioned to provide constructive feedback. I need to emphasise that I do not give special issue editors a quota of manuscripts that they can accept: if a manuscript deserves to be accepted it should be accepted. On occasion, we have allocated the accepted special issue articles across two consecutive issues because there were so many excellent articles to publish. In contrast, if only a

---

[1] https://onlinelibrary.wiley.com/page/journal/13652575/homepage/special_issues.htm
[2] https://onlinelibrary.wiley.com/page/journal/16814835/homepage/specialissues

single article makes it through the review process, then the special issue will consist of just that one article.

The guest editors of the special issue have full responsibility to ensure that a rigorous review process is followed. While I act as a tough gatekeeper with regard to vetting a special issue proposal, once my approval has been given I generally try not to interfere with the management of the special issue, unless I am editing it myself. The exception is when special issue guest editors violate my trust in them. This happened twice with journals I edit. On one occasion, the special issue editors accepted manuscripts without having had them reviewed at all. Some of these manuscripts were actually written by the special issue editors themselves, a practice that I specifically forbid. On another occasion, the special issue editor refused to respond to any email communications from myself (as EinC) and failed to put in place any kind of rigorous review process. In both of these situations I cancelled the special issue entirely. All manuscripts that had been accepted were put back into a regular review process, with myself as SE. In the end, we accepted two of them, as regular research articles. The rest were all rejected. A less serious, but more common, problem with special issues is that the guest SEs and AEs are unfamiliar with the culture of the journal that is hosting the special issue. This lack of familiarity could mean that the rigour of the review process is inadequate, with the result that the accepted articles fail to meet the quality threshold for the journal. It could also mean that the journal's expectations with regard to timeliness are not upheld. For instance, if the guest SEs and AEs unreasonably delay making decisions on submitted manuscripts, this may damage the reputation of the journal itself. In one case, I found that all the guest SEs and AEs had allowed deadlines to slip by as much as 2 months. When I reminded them, they found a number of 'reasons' to excuse their behaviour, but could not make any commitment to identify a date when they would be able to complete the delayed tasks.

Following these experiences, I created a detailed set of guidelines for special issues. These describe both what we expect to see in a proposal for a special issue, and the standards of behaviour that we expect of special issue guest editors. Key points in these guidelines relate to the identification of suitably skilled guest SEs and AEs, including the strong preference that at least one of the SEs and several of the AEs already be working as an SE or AE at the same journal (note: regular AEs are allowed to be guest SEs). With respect to skills, I require that guest SEs and AEs have already established an international reputation in the discipline area, and should have the authority, credibility and experience to make impartial decisions about submitted manuscripts. Scholars who have not published in the journal for which they are proposing a special issue, or a journal of similar calibre, are likely to find that their proposals are rejected. I do not normally allow a person to be a guest SE for more than one special issue concurrently so as to avoid the situation where one person has too much control over the articles that are accepted for publication. I insist that initial submission deadlines should never be extended, but at the same time require that deadlines be set at least 6 months into the future, so that prospective authors have sufficient time to craft a high-quality submission. Adhering to deadlines is important not only for authors, but also for reviewers, AEs and SEs.

Guest SEs are not permitted to submit a manuscript to their own special issue in any authorial capacity. Violation of this rule will lead to immediate rejection of the manuscript and termination of the guest SE status. Guest AEs are permitted, and indeed encouraged, to submit manuscripts to a special issue that they are associated with for several reasons. Firstly, I want to encourage expert authors to serve as AEs so as to facilitate the review process. If serving AEs are not allowed to submit, they might rather not be AEs at all. Further, I see no conflict of interest because an AE will obviously not be the AE for their own manuscript, yet are well-positioned to identify potential reviewers. I need to emphasise that the review process for a special issue is not a zero-sum game. It makes no sense for an AE to reject a manuscript in order to increase the chance that their own manuscript will be accepted, for the simple reason that special issues do not have a quota of manuscripts that can be accepted, as mentioned above. When a special issue is complete, the guest SEs are required to write up an editorial introduction. In this they can provide an overview of the field, as well as an introduction to the articles accepted for publication. This editorial introduction should not include original empirical research, but it can include an agenda for future research directions.

4.5 Sourcing Excellence

All authors are expected to conform to basic standards of excellence in their research. We provide detailed guidelines for authors that have been customised to the specific journal. A sample of these guidelines can be found here.[3] These guidelines start off with a short introduction to the journal and also point authors to selected editorials that may help them position their work for the journal. We document the manuscript types that we accept, and describe each type succinctly. While most manuscripts submitted to journals are

---

[3] https://onlinelibrary.wiley.com/page/journal/13652575/homepage/forauthors.html

classified as 'Research Articles', other prominent manuscript types are: Research Notes, Opinions, Practitioner Articles, Editorials, Commentaries, Book Reviews and Letters to the Editor. Some journals may allow more specialised manuscript types like Debates, Commentaries and Research Method Articles. For instance, at *EJISDC* we specifically request that authors should situate their research designs in the developing country context. We may also identify the manuscript types or topics or styles that we discourage. It is good to make this information clear at the outset so as to reduce the likelihood that authors submit wholly inappropriate manuscripts. However, not all authors read the guidelines and I find that I often reject manuscripts that are out of scope for this reason. We also provide information on formatting standards, proofing, ethics, publication charges and the cost of making an accepted article available on an open access basis. I discuss issues surrounding open access in more detail in Chap. 8.

4.6 Sourcing Authors and Their Motivations

The final point to make about the sourcing of appropriate content relates to what motivates authors to undertake research in the first place. We have observed that many researchers motivate their research by identifying a 'gap' in the literature and claim that because no one has done this research before, so they are going to be the first ones to do it. Gap-spotting research has been demonstrated as having severe limitations (Alvesson and Sandberg 2011), not least because gaps are often uninteresting or unimportant, and as an alternative we suggest that researchers should problematise their research (Chatterjee and Davison 2021). The essence of problematisation is to question prior assumptions and challenge previously established findings. Even as researchers stand on the shoulders of giants, they should not be in awe of those giants, no matter how famous they are (cf. Bacon 1620). One way to engage in a critique is to demonstrate how prior research restricts our understanding of a phenomenon. The researcher can then explain how a new approach, perhaps with a new theory or method, will enable new insights to be gleaned. For instance, we encourage researchers to think indigenously: what are the local or indigenous contextual factors that influence a situation or phenomenon. We hope that they will include these local factors in their research design. A lot of prior research has been undertaken by researchers who are located in North America or Western Europe. But there are many other regions of the world where different cultural values may apply and different indigenous concepts may significantly influence how people behave. Theorising these indigenous concepts can lead to new research directions that significantly contribute to knowledge.

Are these the kind of contributions that EinCs would like to see in submitted research manuscripts? If yes, then the EinC may need to encourage them explicitly, giving researchers the confidence that these indigenous research designs and contributions will be valued. For instance, in our guidelines for authors we specifically indicate that we like to see novel attempts at theorisation, including indigenous theorisation, and provide links to articles that we have already published that make such contributions. We have previously organised a special issue with a focus on indigenous theorisation, with accepted articles describing indigenous theories situated in China, New Zealand and South Africa. We have also organised special issues with a regional geographic focus, viz.: the Balkans, ASEAN (Association of South East Asian Nations) countries, China, Latin America and Africa.

5

Encouraging Great Reviewing Practices

Abstract This chapter focuses on the issues associated with developing an appropriate culture and process for the reviewing of manuscripts. Consistent reviewing practices contribute to the reputation of a journal in ways that will help to establish its reputation. Editors need to consider very carefully what kinds of reviewer behaviour they seek to encourage or discourage. For instance, at the journals I edit I emphasise the importance of constructive reviewing that is critical and thorough, yet also polite. Getting the right tone of the language that is used to communicate with different stakeholders is critical, and warrants careful attention.

Next to sourcing the submission of high-quality manuscripts, an equally important task for the EinC is ensuring that an appropriate peer review process is in place (Lee 1995). Peer review, for all its limitations, is one of the hallmarks of academic publishing (see Davison et al. (2005) for a historical and contemporary perspective of peer review). The peer review process is important because it helps to ensure that the manuscripts accepted for publication have met the expectations of the authors' peers, broadly defined, within the disciplinary area. This 'meeting of expectations' is a summative euphemism for a variety of attributes, but primarily: conforming to expected standards of research conduct, including appropriate analyses of data, contributions to theory and practice, scholarly writing, referencing and formatting; and demonstrating that the research itself was undertaken in a methodologically rigorous way, in accordance with the ethical expectations appropriate to the discipline and journal. In Chap. 2, I wrote at some length about the communication processes that EinCs engage in. Many of these communications relate to the peer review process. In this chapter I focus less on the communication and more on the peer review process itself.

5.1 Creating the Reviewing Culture and Process

The EinC of a long-established journal may find, on appointment, that a comprehensive review system and culture is firmly in place. In contrast, the first EinC of a new journal may find that there is no review system or culture in place. The activities and values that I describe in this chapter are more likely to be of value to EinCs in journals where the peer review system is less well developed, or where the EinC has concerns about current review practices. Nevertheless, even the EinCs of journals that have long-established peer review processes may find some value. There is no single best way to manage a peer review process and even after many years as an EinC, I occasionally introduce modifications to the process, often informed by the processes in place at peer journals.

Once a submitted manuscript has been screened in by the EinC or ME, i.e. found suitable for entering the peer review process, the EinC assigns the manuscript to an SE who contacts an AE and later reviewers. Confirming the participation of peer reviewers is much harder than it appears. In the last few years, I have found that to secure two competent reviewers we may have to invite 20: the vast majority decline or ignore the invitation. Some journals allow authors to nominate potential reviewers. I personally find this to be helpful, as authors often know who are the experts in their field and are thus well placed to identify potential reviewers. The MMS may also identify potential reviewers, though I find that the algorithms are often poorly written with the result that the recommended reviewers are rarely appropriate and so I tend to ignore them altogether.

So long as there are no conflicts of interest, I am generally happy for one of the author-nominated reviewers to be invited. We ask authors not to nominate people where there are conflicts of interest, but it is sensible to check, not least because conflicts of interest are not always apparent: the person who identifies and invites reviewers needs to check that the identified reviewers don't work at the same institution as the authors, are not recent (last 5 years) co-authors, or otherwise compromised. For instance, I have seen a situation where the reviewer team included (a) the husband of the author, (b) the former advisor/supervisor of the author and (c) the former PhD student of the author, all for the same submission. Fortunately, the former supervisor and former PhD student declined the invitation to review. The husband's review turned out to be critical, albeit positive, and the submitted manuscript was rejected after review, but it was a good lesson for me, as well as the SE and AE handling the manuscript.

However, it is not practical for the EinC to monitor all reviewer assignments. At many journals, hundreds of manuscripts may be in the peer review process at any one time with many hundreds or thousands of reviewers involved. Micromanaging this process for all submissions would be immensely time consuming: instead, it is better that the EinC trusts the SEs and AEs to do a good job. In my experience, people appreciate that trust and, with rare exceptions, undertake their work to the very highest standards.

Once the identity of potential reviewers has been confirmed, it is time to invite them by email. I prefer to contact them individually and through private email to invite them to review before assigning the manuscript to them. If the reviewer already has an account in the MMS, the manuscript can be assigned directly. If the reviewer does not have an account, then an account can be created but it is better to do this with the permission of the person concerned, i.e. after the person has agreed to be a reviewer. I get a lot of invitations to review manuscripts from journals (and editors) that I have never heard of, where the editor has created an account for me (without my permission) and then assigned me to be a reviewer of the manuscript. I consider this to be both a violation of my privacy and presumptuous of my acceptance of the invitation. I often decline these invitations, but my account remains and I may be invited again in future. I then need to ask the editor to remove my account, which they may be unwilling or unable to do. If the editor had asked me in advance if I would be willing to review a manuscript with X title and Y abstract, then my declining would not lead to a new account being created. I certainly do not want to log into an MMS (where I will need to create a username and password) simply in order to delete my account.

The invitation email contains details of the manuscript itself (title and abstract) as well as detailed guidelines where we outline our expectations regarding the nature of the review that we hope to receive. Potential reviewers can accept or decline the invitation to review by clicking on a link that takes them either to a log in page for the MMS or direct to the manuscript (in the case of invitation acceptance), or to a text box (in the case of invitation declination) where they can explain why they decline to review and whom they believe may be suitable alternate reviewers. Ideally, reviewers will read and internalise the guidelines that we indicate before they start to read the manuscript and write up their review. The guidelines often vary from journal to journal and we include a check box in the review form that asks 'Did you read the reviewer guidelines?', but there is no way to enforce the reading. Indeed, some reviewers may object to these strictures, asserting their academic freedom to write the review howsoever they like. The guidelines amount to a policy document[1] that encapsulates how we want the peer review process to be applied. Adhering to these guidelines helps us to ensure that accepted articles are of an appropriately high standard, with lower quality manuscripts weeded out, and authors facilitated to achieve a standard of contribution that they might not be able to achieve alone.

Considerable trust is placed in reviewers, but also considerable responsibility. We require that they create a review that is critical, thorough and trenchant, yet also developmental, helpful and constructive. We expect that reviewers will be fair, impartial, open-minded and unbiased. We appreciate that they write in a style that is polite and that they complete their review by the deadline. Achieving a review that manifests these outcomes often requires some degree of assistance since reviewers do not always possess the necessary characteristics. Unfortunately, a few may see their role as mere 'reject agents'. Rarely, I have come across reviewers and AEs who 'proudly' informed me that they had never recommended acceptance of a single manuscript for a particular journal. Beyond this extreme case, I find that reviewers are often biased for or against specific forms of research and thus their selection must be handled with care (Davison 2014). The editor, often the AE, who directly contacts the reviewer, needs to set up the right set of expectations for the review. If the submitted review is inadequate in some dimension, the AE may need to rescind the review, i.e. return it to the reviewer, with an explanation of what needs to be corrected. The reviewer may then edit the review and resubmit it. Rarely we may expunge their reviews altogether, essentially removing the reviewer from the entire review process. Here our duty of care for authors is paramount. We need to avoid the situation that was related to me by a senior colleague, who observed 'I sense that some reviewers are reading the manuscript for openings they can use to spew out their own thoughts on the matter, to show off their own genius, or simply to exercise their personality disorders'.

5.2 Characteristics of the Culture and the Reviewers

As EinC, I fully appreciate the dichotomous obligations of publishing high-quality articles that collectively advance knowledge, and of helping authors to write those same articles via an effective peer review process. I believe that it is

---

[1] See for instance: https://onlinelibrary.wiley.com/page/journal/13652575/homepage/for-reviewers

essential for the review process to be constructive and developmental if it is to be at all effective. Reviewers thus have the duty to offer honest critique that offers a way out of a problem situation. Naturally reviewers should identify flaws and faults in the application of method or theory, in analysis and argument. It may be that these flaws are fatal, i.e. they cannot be rectified in the current study without either a new research design or new data or both. Such errors might exist because some literature has been ignored, or some more recent standards or findings have not been incorporated, or because the argumentative logic is inadequate. Even when faced with such a calamitous situation, a reviewer can be constructive by pointing the authors towards resources with which they need to familiarise themselves.

It is easy to be a critical reviewer who finds fault with (almost) everything that is written. Such critical reviewers are not necessarily evil nor do they always suffer from personality disorders, though it may seem like that to the author. Nevertheless, to find fault with everything and to appreciate nothing is not simply a matter of developing a reputation for toughness. It is also brutish and merciless. Some of the toughest and least forgiving reviews I have seen were written by PhD students who lack the practical experience of research, yet have a wealth of knowledge gleaned in the classroom. Some of the kindest and most sympathetic reviews that I have seen were crafted by more experienced researchers who know just how hard it is to do good research, who understand fully that perfect research is a chimera, who are experts at seeking the glints and facets of contributions and then helping authors to bring them into view.

A real danger of excessively tough reviews is that the authors will walk away and try elsewhere, with the result that the manuscript is 'lost'. This happens occasionally at the journals I edit, and yet we have also benefitted from the same happening at other journals. In 2019, I was talking to an author who shared that his manuscript had just been given a 'major revision' decision for the fifth time at a premier journal because one reviewer was holding out for more changes. The authors essentially gave up: they did not want to make any more changes. In 2022, I had a similar conversation with authors who objected to the line of argument taken by an SE on the third round of review. They felt that the SE was trying, at much too late a stage, to change the orientation of the research. As a result, they decided not to revise the manuscript at all, but to withdraw it from the journal. In both of these cases, I encouraged the authors to submit their manuscripts to one of the journals I edit and both manuscripts were accepted after one more round of minor revisions. They went on to be highly cited, which amounts to a loss for the journals to which they were previously submitted, but a gain for the journal that published them and indeed for the discipline.

It's fair to point out that some EinCs do have the policy that all reviewers must be satisfied before a manuscript can be accepted, but achieving such a high level of consensus is very tricky. Not only are some reviewers apparently unable to commit to a recommendation of acceptance, but they may have opinions diametrically opposed to those of other reviewers. How can the author address both? What sometimes happens is that when one reviewer is satisfied, this reviser will not see the revised manuscript again. The authors can then make the changes needed to satisfy the other reviewer(s), even though these changes may violate the expectations of the first reviewer. Such a situation is plainly ludicrous, yet it happens if all reviewers must (at some stage) recommend acceptance.

In contrast, I strongly believe that the EinC is the one person who has the prerogative to decide and should enact that responsibility more often. In practice, as EinC I almost invariably accept and put into effect the recommendation of the SE. I trust the SE, who is often much more of an expert in the topic area than I am. However, as I have mentioned elsewhere, I do not see the review process as being an inherently democratic one: in my view, reviewers make recommendations. They do not vote. Their recommendations are not binding. The AE should naturally reflect on those recommendations, but is not bound by them. The AE must also form an independent opinion, informed by the recommendations. The SE will consider both the AE's opinion and the reviewers' recommendations. But when the AE in essence says 'Do everything that the reviewers ask for' and offers no additional guidance, then the AE is not doing their job. The situation is compounded if the SE follows the same line of reasoning.

As a corollary to the above concern about overly critical reviewers, I recognise that PhD students and junior scholars in particular may feel under considerable pressure to turn in high quality, critical reviews out of a concern that their own reputation as researchers is being assessed by the AE, SE or EinC. This amounts to an unpleasant conundrum: 'I want to help the authors, but I also want to help myself. Can I do both?'. My advice to reviewers in this situation is 'Yes, you can do both, if you are careful, and if you want to do both'. The old adage about sowing the wind and reaping the whirlwind comes to mind here: if you as a reviewer are unduly critical, you can expect that you will get unduly critical reviews of your own manuscripts in future. You can break this mould by being generous even as you are critical. It is true that editors do evaluate the quality of a review but there are many attributes to quality. Being nasty is not one of them! We expect that reviewers will be critical, especially in early rounds of a review process. We also expect them to be constructive, friendly and even caring. Building your reputation as a fair but competent reviewer will take time, but you will be noticed and an AE invitation may come your way. The very best reviewers are recognised publicly with 'best reviewer of the year' awards.

I particularly value the reviewer who is open-minded about a new research area and prepared to devote significant time to crafting a review that is manifestly fair, impartial and unbiased. However, finding such open-minded reviewers is by no means an easy task. The vast majority of potential reviewers tend to be experts in rather narrow areas and are often unwilling to venture far outside their comfort zones. The people who are perhaps best suited to act as reviewers in these cases are the members of the EAB, themselves senior scholars who should be more familiar with a variety of topics, methods, theories and epistemological positions.

The final attributes of a good review that I want to emphasise relate to it being on time and written in a polite and friendly style. Each journal will have its own standard expectations for timeliness and these are generally communicated to potential reviewers when they are first invited. The amount of time offered ranges from a few weeks to a couple of months. A reviewer who accepts the invitation to review is also accepting the deadline by when to complete the review. Keeping to the deadline is critical and it is the AE's, SE's or EinC's job to contact reviewers who fail to do so, which unfortunately occurs all too often. Indeed, it is not unusual for a review to be a month or more overdue and for every communication from editor to reviewer to be studiously ignored. What can the editor do? You could try sending emails every day, ideally at different times of day, so as to remind the reviewer again and again that their review is still expected and will be gratefully received. If you know someone at the same institution, you could try to find out if there are any special circumstances that are relevant: perhaps the reviewer is sick, or is no longer employed there, or there are other reasons why your message is not being received. But you need to be careful not to reveal any personal information to your helper. You may also want to make sure that this individual is not invited to review again. There are ways to arrange this in most MMS. Talk to your publisher.

5.3 Tone and Register: How to Get the Language Right

Judging the tone of language used in a review is an art in itself. It is easy to be too direct and the reviewer may not appreciate the impact of the words on the author. For instance, some reviewers write 'You did this, you said that', when they could write 'The authors say this or do that'. Is there a difference? In my view, this is as much about style as anything. Personally, I find it anthropomorphic to write 'The manuscript says' because manuscripts don't say anything. They are not human and only humans can say things (AI apart). However, one of the reviewers of this book commented:

> I find that one of the most offensive things that reviewers do mindlessly is to write the review as if it were a critique of the author, not the manuscript. For example, they say "you say" when they mean "the manuscript says". The number of times I have edited reviews to replace "you" with "the manuscript" is a large fraction of the number of new reviewers I've used. I always tell them I've done this, but I do not ask their permission. Mostly they don't do it twice. If they do it a second time, they've shown themselves to be bullies, and they're off my list.

Well, I fervently respect this reviewer, but I sincerely disagree. I suspect that this disagreement is stylistic. I don't find it to be at all offensive, let alone bullying, to use 'you' instead of 'the manuscript'. I mean, it is 'you' (the author) because only the author is responsible for the words that the author uses (unless they are relying on generative AI, but that's a different matter). So, when I, as a reviewer, write 'you say', I don't mean 'the manuscript says'; I really mean 'you say' because you did say! Further, I sincerely object to an editor unilaterally editing a review so as to conform with the editor's view of a correct style. If an editor did this to me as reviewer, I would courteously refuse to review for that editor again! Nevertheless, the larger point remains that one has to judge the tone of the review with great care. If you find my own stance offensive but don't want to write 'the manuscript says' then you may need to create a more circuitous form of words along the lines of 'In the manuscript, I read that …' or 'The authors appear to make the case that …'. Beyond these instances of style, it is good practice to show your completed review to a colleague *before* submitting it. This will help you to get some perspective and avoid inadvertently hurting the author or annoying the editor.

The directness of communication is as much a cultural attribute as a personal one: direct communication is valued more in some cultures than others. EinCs in particular need to develop skills in diplomatic communication when interacting with authors and reviewers (Davison 2017b). Techatassanasoontorn and Davison (2022) write at length about this communication and suggest that it can usefully take the form of a scholarly conversation between authors and reviewers. Some authors seem reluctant to have the conversation at all because they just want to do everything that the review team asks for, no matter how ridiculous or even contradictory it may be! This is sad, and from my point of view a missed opportunity. There will always be situations where the authors should push back against the suggestions of the review team and explain that they undertook their research or described a situation in a particular way entirely deliberately, and do not wish to change it. Provided that the arguments are reasonable and well-grounded, the review team should have the common sense and simple decency to accept such arguments. As the SE of a journal recently wrote to me (in my role as author): 'I actually don't expect that you will do all these things. Feel free to explain why you think that they are unnecessary. But, please do engage with all our comments. Let's have a conversation'.

On the other hand, conversations with authors can sometimes be difficult and require particular tact. For instance, imagine the situation where the authors not-so-politely reject all your carefully considered remarks and insist that their way of presenting an argument is the only one that they deem appropriate. Further, they claim that as you (the EinC) are not familiar with their precise context and they (the authors) are, so you have no right to suggest changes to their manuscript. In such a situation (and this scenario is modified from a recent real case) it is simple to reject the manuscript on the basis that the authors are unwilling or unable to revise to the satisfaction of the review team. But that's really too easy. The reason why the manuscript was sent for review was because it has an important message. As EinC, I was grateful that the authors entrusted the journal with their manuscript. The challenge is to persuade the authors to convey that message in a way that is accessible to the wider audience of the journal, and necessarily that means that some revisions may be needed. In this particular case, I created a review team of people who were broadly sympathetic to the ideas being expressed, who came from the same demographic segment as the authors, who could relate to the authors (even if I, as EinC, could not) and indeed who self-identified their demographic characteristics in their reviews. Faced with this information, the authors toned down their rejection of the review comments and agreed to make some substantive changes, though not as many as I had hoped for. While the process was at times awkward, it was, at least on my side, always diplomatic. The outcome was not ideal, but it was good enough. I hope that the authors learned from this experience. If you recognise yourself as an author who has had this kind of conversation with an editor or review team, I invite you to reflect on the situation: put yourself in the shoes of the reviewers, AE, SE or EinC, and try to understand what their role entails.

5.4 Peer Review Roles

In the final part of this chapter, I explore roles related to peer review. The SEs and AEs play very significant roles, which implies that they need to take their roles seriously! I have come across SEs and AEs who appear to imagine that they are entitled to the role, but do little to enact their responsibilities. This is clearly unacceptable. Tarafdar and Davison (2021) explore the SE and AE roles in considerable detail, highlighting the behaviour of an exemplary SE or AE. AEs are not the final decision-makers, even though SEs may be, but they are closely connected to the review process. They know who the authors are and they need to demonstrate a high degree of care in how they manage the peer review process. They have the right to desk reject a manuscript if they believe that this is appropriate. They also have the responsibility to select as many suitable reviewers as they deem necessary. Very often two reviewers are selected, but three or four may be required on some occasions. As EinC, I prefer to trust people: I have confidence to delegate the peer review process to the SEs and AEs, knowing that the manuscript is in good hands, the hands of people I trust. When reviews come in, the SE and AE need to reach a decision. Ideally this is consensual, and there is transparent communication between them, but this is not always possible and split opinions within the review team are not unusual. I need to emphasise that the reviewers and SEs/AEs are offering thoughts and making recommendations. The reviewers (hopefully) have provided a trenchant analysis of the manuscript, assessing its strengths and weaknesses. The AE should have read those reviews and in addition provided his/her own opinion. The SE should do likewise. The SE's recommendation is usually final, since it is rare that the EinC disagrees with the SE, and at some journals it is the SE who communicates directly with the authors.

6

Developing and Maintaining an Audience

Abstract Chapter 6 examines the audience of the journal. Here I explore steps that the editor can take to grow the audience of a journal, in both academic and non-academic spheres. For instance, while the audience might almost be taken for granted, journals often serve particular niches and so it may be valuable to target niches, both in terms of the willingness of these people to submit their research, but also to read and cite articles published in the journal. An audience that is not always associated with the academic journal is made up of practitioners or other nonacademics. Reaching this audience is harder if the articles published are not seen as useful, which thus constitutes a challenge for the editor: is the journal open to the publication of articles that will appeal more to a practitioner audience?

As a journal's reputation and stature in its field evolves, it will become famous or even notorious for its publication of certain types of article. For instance, certain topics might be identified as inside or outside the scope of the journal, and so might certain approaches to research. Journals can also be recognised for their cultural values and the kinds of research that they encourage. Editorials that are published in the journal may be sought after and cited in their own right. If the journal is promoted not only via the publisher's website but also via a list serve or social media platform, then it may attract a more visible crowd of loyal followers eager to promote and defend it, as the circumstances dictate. Thus, there are different ways in which the EinC can develop and maintain the journal's audience. Proactive EinCs can leverage the different channels to ensure that the audience is kept up to date with new developments, opportunities and feedback to questions that are submitted.

Although the broad audience for the journal might include anyone working in the wider discipline, the EinC may wish to target a more specific audience of people who see the journal as either the preferred outlet for their own research or indeed as a primary source of ideas. A few years ago, I wrote to a variety of scholars in my field to ask firstly, for whom they are writing (Davison 2019) and secondly, how do they select a journal to submit to (Davison 2020a). Each of these questions relates to the audience of the journal, though in different ways. The questions were prompted by a concern I had that some authors may only write in order to satisfy reviewers, neglecting the real stakeholders with whom they wanted to communicate, i.e. the audience that reads the journal to which they submitted the manuscript. As an author myself, I know that I select a journal because of its audience, and there are some journals in my own discipline that I would never willingly submit to for precisely the same reason: I am not writing for those journals' audiences. Unless the journal publishes research in a tiny niche field, it is likely that the potential audience is at least several hundred people, and possibly thousands or tens of thousands. The more popular or famous publications may attract millions of readers. Many journals collect data on how many times an article has been downloaded. Scopus,[1] the Web of Science,[2] and Google Scholar[3] offer similar metrics, showing how many cites each published article has received, and thus gauge the size of the audience; EinCs can do the same, as Google Scholar offers journal level metrics.[4]

Ten scholars responded to my first question, viz.: 'when you write a research article, for whom are you writing?'. I organised their answers about the nature of the audience into three categories: the readers, the reviewers and the self. For instance, one of my respondents who focused on readers wrote 'If I'm writing for an IS audience … then I make sure that the problem statement is one that IS people would find interesting'. Another opined similarly: 'When I write a manuscript for first time submission, I write for the readership of a given journal that publishes the type of research I'm interested in pursuing'. He also commented 'I'm writing about something that I care about, for readers that I suspect also care about that area of knowledge. I'll try to engage with the on-going conversation at the selected journal as much as possible'. In contrast, another respondent wrote 'I believe that many or most seasoned

---

[1] http://www.scopus.com
[2] https://clarivate.com/products/scientific-and-academic-research/research-discovery-and-workflow-solutions/webofscience-platform/
[3] https://scholar.google.com/
[4] https://scholar.google.com/citations?view_op=metrics_intro&hl=en

researchers write with reviewers in mind, if not for the first submission, then certainly by the third revision. In fact, the exasperation is so great by the third or fourth revision that the general audience has completely disappeared from the author's mind and the author is left just wanting to address what the reviewers and editor want'. Others offer more moderate views, such as 'The message I want to convey is non-negotiable [yet] I have to admit that a couple of times my original message has been substantially changed along the way to satisfy reviewers' comments'. In a recent conversation with a different author, I learned that the authors refused to revise a manuscript for a top journal, even though only minor revisions were required, because those revisions would take the manuscript in a different direction to the one that they wanted. They thus decided to withdraw the manuscript and send it elsewhere. As an example of authors who seemed to write for themselves, one scholar noted 'I do not typically write the first version for the reviewers or the editor. Rather I write for myself. I ask myself whether the text is the most convincing, aesthetically pleasing and true account that I can give'.

A different group of ten scholars responded to my second question, viz.: 'Ignoring questions of ranking and any list of preferred journals that your department may prefer you to publish in, what are the characteristics of a journal that you (as a potential author) identify as contributing to its relevance or appropriateness as an outlet for your research?'. Here, I wanted to explore the audience at the journal level not the manuscript level. My interest was premised on my assumption that each journal exists in what I characterise as a 'self-spun web' of intellectual engagement (cf. Green et al. 2009), and that this web is associated with a specific population of people who read, review for and submit to the journal. This is relevant to the EinC because it is not hard to imagine a situation where the 'self-spun web' falls out of favour with an audience, for instance if it is seen as being out of touch with contemporary research trends. This may then lead to declining downloads (which will worry the publisher), falling submission numbers (which will worry the EinC), problems in securing reviewers (who perhaps don't want to be associated with the journal, even vicariously, which will also worry the EinC), and perhaps the ultimate existential crisis: nothing to publish and therefore no reason to exist. If such a state of affairs seems likely to develop, the EinC needs to consider repositioning the journal as a matter of priority, with a radical change in the 'self-spun web' such that it is aligned with the interests of a sufficiently broad or diverse population of readers and authors. Such a repositioning would require extensive consultation with the journal's many stakeholders, not least the publisher. Indeed, the publisher might well prefer to see a different EinC at the helm.

My respondents to the question that I pose above had a variety of perspectives. Some indicated that they submit to a journal because of the reputation of the editors, authors who have published there previously and the publisher. For instance, one of my interlocutors noted that he checks to see if 'reputable scholars are on the editorial board as SEs and AEs, and whether the board is diverse in terms of research expertise'. Others wrote that they select journals that are well recognized for having fast review and publication cycle times, as well as for 'providing high-quality, constructive, and timely reviewer comments'. Other than these reputational facets, the nature of the journal's audience is also important: one respondent noted that she selects journals whose readers she is trying to influence. 'She wants those people to read her work and change what they do because of what she says. As a result, she only publishes in venues where she thinks those people will read her articles'. Another commented that he 'would like to find an audience that will find the contribution of the article relevant and helpful'.

The question of the audience also arises when a journal is hijacked by an interest group which tries to reposition the journal in such a way that it, more or less exclusively, meets the needs of the interest group with little regard for anyone else's interests. This shift is certainly easier to effect if the EinC is also the hijacker-in-chief and the impact will be all the greater if the EinC has many years of tenure left to run. Such a hijacking EinC can readily reorient the journal and its ethos in a radically new direction that may be of interest to a very different population than was previously the case. If sufficient numbers of authors and readers can be persuaded to sign up for this new direction, then the hijacking may be successful, even as other authors decide to shun the journal altogether. If the journal is highly ranked, however, the larger audience who are not interested in the new direction may be significantly annoyed that their research is excluded and this journal is essentially out of reach. They may not only stop reading the journal, but also refuse to review for it or even cite it. Over time, the ranking of the journal may change with a falling impact factor and even public ostracism that is visible in such actions as refusing to invite the EinC to panels at conferences where EinCs discuss the issues of the discipline.

At any time, the EinC may also try to reach out to new audiences. Special issues can be one way to achieve this. The focus on a new topic that lies outside the normal scope of the journal may bring authors who have never submitted to the journal before, but who may be encouraged to submit manuscripts on a more regular basis in future. A different approach is to target an audience who have never even noticed the journal before. For instance, with respect to the journals I edit, over the last decade I have championed practitioner papers. These are intended to be manuscripts that are written either exclusively by, and for, practitioners, or are co-authored by academics and practitioners, yet still with practitioners as the primary audience. When we created the practitioner paper submission type, we also prepared a detailed description of what this kind of manuscript should look like. For instance, we emphasised the need to offer a practitioner perspective in a specific context and to contribute insights that will be of interest to practitioners in solving practical problems and challenges. We clearly indicated that we do not expect a theoretical contribution in a practitioner-oriented manuscript. We also pointed out that we do not expect senior managers to constitute the only audience. Practitioners at any level could be the audience. In order to handle practitioner-oriented manuscripts appropriately, I have recruited SEs and AEs who have the requisite skills and sensitivity to both the genre and the journal. The entire initiative has been warmly welcomed by the publisher because it enables us to target a hitherto barely tapped market of authors and readers. Academics who work closely with practitioners are also interested in the opportunity, and they too have submitted high-quality work.

Problematisation (cf. Chatterjee and Davison 2021) is a key concept in all research manuscripts, including practitioner-oriented manuscripts. Instead of spotting a gap in the literature, we encourage authors to motivate their study with a real problem that affects practitioner stakeholders and that has not been adequately investigated previously. Insights obtained through the conduct of practitioner-oriented research have the potential to create significant impact for organisations and their employees, but also for a local community like a village, a non-profit, or the environment. In the 14 years since we first welcomed practitioner-oriented manuscripts, 65 have been submitted and 5 have been accepted, i.e. 7.7%, which is comparable with the acceptance rate of regular research articles. Practitioners write to us to ask about the possibility of publication and with the flourishing of executive programmes like the Doctor of Business Administration (DBA), there is increasing interest from practitioners in burnishing their credentials with a publication in a scholarly journal.

Audiences are supposedly fickle, willing to change their loyalty at the click of a mouse. In my experience, the audience's loyalty can be secured if their interests are served. At the journals I edit, the data suggests that this loyalty is strong: we have increasing numbers of both submissions and downloads. As a result, we are able to publish more high-quality articles that are of interest to a wider audience. Special issues certainly contribute to this: at the time of writing, one of the journals I edit has 16 special issues in progress, each representing a niche area that can attract new authors to submit a regular manuscript to the journal in the future.

7

Developing and Maintaining a Reputation

Abstract In this chapter, I consider the reputation of the journal, and the way this reputation can be enhanced, or damaged. This topic is closely related to Chapter 6 because the reputation to a significant extent depends on the way the audience sees the journal. Reputation is not only a matter of benchmarking with other journals. It also involves being known for the publication of specific research topics, or research of a particular genre. For instance, as already described in Chapter 5, a key objective for the journals I edit is that they be known for the constructiveness of the reviewing arrangements. I regard this as a key element in the reputation of those journals.

As I discussed in the previous chapter, the audience of a journal will be concerned about its reputation. Reputation is quite a subjective notion and can vary across such different demographic segments as countries, methods, topics and, I suspect, even ethnicity. Thus, a journal that has an excellent reputation among the members of one demographic segment may have a much less impressive reputation among the members of a different demographic segment, often because the two groups use different criteria to evaluate the same journal. For instance, my colleagues in South Africa often rate very highly those journals that are free to access, because they don't have the financial resources to pay for access to paywalled journals. Scholars in other countries may use a very different yardstick, referring to the journal's inclusion on a particular index or its impact factor. Given these competing expectations, and the unlikelihood that any journal can be rated as excellent on all criteria by all populations of stakeholders, an EinC needs to determine which population the journal sets out to be appreciated by, and thus who the submitting authors are likely to be.

If a journal is already well-established, then it is likely to have a reputation already among its target population. Maintaining or incrementally enhancing this reputation is probably not too difficult, provided that standards are upheld, and the interests of the audience are fulfilled. However, I have seen several cases where a reputation changed markedly because of a change in editorial policy, and not always for the better.

In the first case, the change of policy came in a society-owned journal where the newly appointed EinC decided (for reasons that are not obvious but may relate to the society's publication committee changing its stance) to modify the requirements imposed on submitting authors. Previously, the journal welcomed authors to submit manuscripts on topics that were broadly in scope, but with quite strict word limits. In the new policy, such submissions were essentially forbidden. The journal moved to a commissioned content only model, where the EinC and other section editors contacted individual people to write commissioned articles. Authors could still self-nominate themselves as potential commissioned content creators, but many were rejected. The consequence of this change was dramatic, with a significant rise in IF but simultaneously a demotion of the journal on journal lists. The rise in IF may relate to the relevance of the new content style for the journal's readers, who presumably found it more appropriate. However, many universities downgraded the journal's reputation because the new sourcing model caused the journal to be out of reach to anyone who was not invited.

In the second case, the change of policy came in a commercially-owned journal where a very long serving EinC stepped down and a much more dynamic EinC was appointed. The new EinC introduced new initiatives, promoted the journal widely, revamped the editorial board with a rich tapestry of prominent and globally located scholars, commissioned content but also managed to increase the number of regular submissions dramatically. The new EinC also instigated a new article type, a multi-authored commentary on an emerging or contemporary topic that was of considerable interest to a very broad audience. These multi-authored commentaries involved 50 or more authors, each of whom was personally invited by the EinC to be an author, yet each person only wrote 500–1000 words. The commentaries were often cited very fast indeed. The net effect of these changes was to cause the impact factor to soar, and given that impact for the journal to be rated very highly by some agencies and universities. While the overall impact on the reputation has been positive, not all scholars are enamoured of the changes, though this may be no more than academic snobbery as the current impact factor is at twice the level of many premier journals that have traditionally had much stronger reputations.

A newly created journal, on the other hand, is likely to experience a very different path towards establishing its reputation. I observe that most new journals take several years to build a reputation, and are highly dependent on the loyalty of their authors and readers. One of the more successful new journals of recent years was formed out of a special interest group in the Management discipline that catered to research about China (Management and Organization Review). The interest group had several hundred members, an active and dynamic leadership team, and was able to persuade a major publisher to take them on. They too commissioned content in the early days, but quickly developed the reputation of being high quality, in part because they were able to access people to act as reviewers and SEs who had previously worked in other premier journals. The new journal was not only affiliated with the special interest group but also with a conference that this interest group organised on a bi-annual basis, which provided an additional source of submissions. They thus created a very visible profile in a sufficiently large niche area with a substantial population of authors and readers who perhaps felt that existing outlets did not meet their needs adequately.

Alas, there are also numerous examples of new journals that have failed to achieve any kind of success or reputation, and the vast majority disappear without trace after a short period of time. In Chap. 4, I recounted the sad story of the *Journal of Failures and Lessons Learned in IT Management*, which folded after only 1 year.

EinCs, most of whom are senior academics, are naturally concerned with the academic side of their role. The stakeholders whom they represent, particularly submitting authors, will be concerned that the quality of accepted articles is high, that the journal maintains or elevates its reputation. Although reputation is subjective, there are relevant measures that can be used as indicative proxies of reputation. For instance, journals are often indexed by third party agencies (such as the Web of Science, Scopus and Google Scholar), and that indexing may serve as a signal to their quality. There are also area-specific indices like the Chartered Association of Business Schools (CABs) Academic Journal Guide, the FT50 list of top journals in business and management, or the Australian Business Dean's Council (ABDC) Journal Quality List.

The impact factor (IF) is a journal-level metric that indicates how well the articles published in that journal are cited, thus signalling indirectly the quality (and reputation) of the journal itself. Davison and Lowry (2023) provide a very extensive analysis of IFs, as well as some recent trends in IF evolution, which I briefly highlight here. Impact factors can be calculated for any period of time, but the most commonly reported period is for the two-year IF. The calculation (for the 2022) IF is as follows:

$$\text{IF}(2022) = \frac{\text{Citations to citable articles published in 2020 and 2021}}{\text{Number of articles published in 2022}}$$

Essentially anything that is published in the two-year period (2020–2021 in the example above) is citable as part of the numerator: research articles, opinions, editorials, book reviews, etc., though not non-academic content such as advertising. The number of articles (denominator) generally refers to a somewhat smaller sub-set as it excludes editorials, book reviews and other non-peer reviewed material. Although a two-year IF is common, it favours journals that publish articles that are quickly cited. In some disciplines, citations take longer to accumulate and so a 5- or 10-year IF may be more appropriate. Meanwhile, Google Scholar calculates an h5 index for journals to indicate a five-year citation trend.[1]

Davison and Lowry (2023) note a number of patterns that are relevant to the EinC who is interested in developing or maintaining a high IF. For instance, they observe that 'the presence of one or more highly cited articles' can skew the IF considerably, especially if the journal publishes a smaller number of articles. They note that in two journals, 41.4% of the 2020 IF and 53.2% of the 2021 IF could be attributed to a single (highly cited) article. They also observe that certain types of articles tend to be more highly cited, notably those that focus: on the development of theory, the promulgation of methods, establishing a research agenda or framework. Articles that deal with contemporary topics are also well cited. Examples include: blockchain, machine learning, artificial intelligence, Covid-19 and digital transformation. However, since in the calculation for a two-year IF there is only a two-year window when the cites to an article are counted, these highly cited articles only exert an impact on the IF for those 2 years, before dropping out of the calculation window. Thus, depending on such highly cited articles for maintaining a high IF requires the frequent publication of such articles.

Davison and Lowry (2023) also look at the polar opposite situation and find that some journals publish significant numbers of articles that are not cited at all during the two-year window. They report how at one journal, some 17.5% of citable articles received no citations at all. High numbers of uncited articles will certainly negatively affect the IF and should be a cause for concern for the EinC. As Davison and Lowry (2023) ask 'Why does one article

---

[1] The h5 index is the largest number of h such that h articles published in the last 5 years have at least h citations each. Here is a link to the 'business, economics and management (general)' research area for 2022: https://scholar.google.com/citations?view_op=top_venues&hl=en&vq=bus_busgeneral. To find a particular journal, such as one not listed in the 20 visible at this link, click the magnifying glass search function at the top right of the page.

languish uncited while another article harvests a rich crop of citations?'. The answer is not always obvious because the journals with stronger reputations do not always have the highest IFs and the articles that may have been developed and improved over many years may be less appreciated than a quick and skimpy analysis of a trendy topic, which is timelier and inherently more interesting. To offer a contemporary example, ChatGPT and other similar Generative AI programmes have occupied popular attention from late 2022 onwards. The first academic articles about them appeared within a few months, and being the first articles, they are highly cited. More careful analyses that may require months or years of painstaking work will appear much later, by which time the topic will have evolved and popular attention will have moved on, reducing the impact of the research and the number of citations received. This also explains why methods articles are often well cited: as long as the methods are still in use, and as long as the article breaks new ground and helps researchers, the potential for it to be cited will be high.

EinCs who hope that their journals' IFs will improve should certainly be concerned about the impact of zero-cited articles, and alert to the opportunities provided by highly cited articles. To some degree, EinCs (and publishers) can game the process by which the IF is calculated by taking advantage of a loophole in the calculation method. As I explain above, the IF for a given year is calculated by counting the number of cites to citable items (numerator) in the two previous years, over the number of published items in that year. However, because the years are calendar years, an article that is published in the January issue of a year will be visible and thus citable for almost a year longer than an article that is published in the December issue of the same year. If an EinC assigns to the first issue(s) of the year the articles that the editor believes are more likely to be cited, and correspondingly the less likely to be cited items to the last issue(s) of the year, then this may have some impact on the citations received in the citation window. The EinC could also skew the distribution of articles across the year, assigning more articles to the earlier issues and fewer articles to the later issues in a given year. Meanwhile, the publisher can also enter the 'spirit' of this game by publishing all articles for a given issue at least on time (not late) or even early. Thus, the January 2025 issue of a journal might be published a few weeks earlier, in December 2024, yet would still count as 2025 because that will be the date that appears on the published articles in that issue. In contrast, a publisher that consistently misses its publication dates will consistently damage its own interests. Finally, a publisher that, perhaps magnanimously or perhaps instrumentally, decides that its first issue of the year should be free to access will find that the articles published in that first issue will have higher download counts and presumably may be more highly cited (all other matters considered) than those not published in the first issue.

As a further corollary to these events, Davison and Lowry (2023) note that the review teams at some journals 'appear to actively encourage authors to cite articles published in the journal to which they are submitting' with correspondingly high self-citation counts. For instance, each of the 13 journals in their data set received more citations from themselves than they received from other sources. The articles published in some journals are cited by a wide range of sources, but the articles published in other journals are cited by a much smaller number of sources. As a result, EinCs must determine which markets they seek to create a reputation in, and thus be cited in, and develop an appropriate strategy to achieve this. A highly reputable journal is likely to serve a significant population of researchers, whether they are in author or reader roles, and as a result it may exert considerable influence over the development of research in the particular field.

Notwithstanding the popularity of IFs, there is also a considerable counter movement to the effect that only article level quality and impact should be measured. An alternative way of assessing quality is at the article level, with metrics like Altmetrics.[2] Here the impact of the article is assessed by examining the extent to which it has been downloaded, read, discussed, recommended and cited. Publication platforms increasingly provide this kind of data as standard so individual authors can track the impact of their research in a more refined way than just looking at an IF, which is a journal level measurement.

An EinC can also enhance the usefulness of the articles published in a journal by curating them into virtual issues that are thematically organised. The virtual issues can be extended as new articles that fit the curation topic become available. These curated collections are valuable for authors as single sources of materials on the same topic. Each curation may be managed by a dedicated editor who also writes up an introduction to the curation and selects articles for inclusion in the curation. Some journals have developed a reputation for this curated content, which likely leads to more downloads and cites of the articles in each curation, which enhances their visibility to the reader population.

Finally, the EinC can build the journal's reputation by developing formal associations with professional associations. Most academic disciplines have professional associations, each of which may recognise the premier or elite journals in their own fields. For example, the *IEEE, ACM, AIS, APA, AAA, IFIP*, etc. If the EinC is able to persuade the professional association to associate itself with the journal, and some incentive might be offered such as discounted access costs for members of the association, then this can singularly raise the visibility of the journal, and, over time, its reputation.

---

[2] http://www.altmetric.com

8

Engaging with the Publisher and Editorial/Production Teams

Abstract This chapter deals with a topic that is largely invisible to both researchers and the audience: engagements with the publisher and the editorial or production teams. Even senior and associate editors may have next to no contact with the publisher. However, the editor of a journal needs to keep in very regular contact with a variety of different people in the publication and editorial offices. These cover both routine and exceptional situations, all of which demand the editor's input and provide opportunities for the editor to exercise a prerogative to make decisions. I explore the challenges and opportunities associated with these types of communication.

An area of the EinC's responsibility that generally lies far from the public view, yet which is central to the activities that the EinC undertakes, concerns the various back-office functions that play a critical role in supporting the journal. These include: the editorial office, where incoming manuscripts are first checked for completeness and are plagiarism-checked before being assigned to the EinC; the production office, which takes care of the process after an article is accepted for publication including copyediting and typesetting; and the publisher's office, where policies are negotiated, the technical staff are located, and strategic directions are initiated. An EinC will need to deal with the personnel in all three offices on a more or less regular basis. Although much of this communication is fairly routine, exceptional situations can also arise.

When a manuscript is submitted, generally via an MMS (though some journals still accept email submissions), it is typically first screened by the

Editorial Assistant (EA), who works in an Editorial Office (EO). One EA typically provides editorial support for many journals from the same publisher. The physical location of the EA/EO varies: the person might work directly for the publisher at one of their offices, but it is more common that the EA/EO is outsourced to a third party provider. For instance, the EA/EO for the two journals that I edit are located in India, yet the offices of the publisher are located in the UK and the USA. It is important to note that the extent to which the publisher finances an EO and thus provides an EA (and some journals may have multiple EAs) varies significantly. While some publishers are very supportive, others provide next to no EO/EA support at all, and the EinC may find that she/he has to handle these matters without any financial support.

Each journal is likely to have a different set of protocols regarding what the EA is required to do when performing the initial screen. It could be as detailed as checking font size, margins, placement of figures and tables, page formatting, reference citation styles, appendices, etc. Some journals allow what is called 'freestyle submission', where the authors can submit in any format they like so long as they format consistently. Other journals have more rigid requirements for particularly formatting style. The protocol may be negotiated with the EinC (or the EinC may be able to modify it) and functions as a way of ensuring that the submitted manuscript is complete and the EinC can process the manuscript easily. However, given that EAs support many journals, each with different protocols, it may happen that for a given manuscript the EA screens it incorrectly and either unnecessarily sends it back to the authors to be revised when revisions are not required or incorrectly assigns it to the EinC when it is in fact not yet ready to be assigned. In the former case, the authors have to undertake further (unnecessary) work and in the latter, the EinC may also have to undertake further work. This initial screening should not take more than 5–10 min for each manuscript for an experienced EA who is familiar with the screening protocol.

A key outcome of the initial screening is the assignment of a unique identification number to each manuscript that will (normally) stay with the manuscript throughout its review journey until a final decision is reached. Examples of manuscript numbers are AA-RA1234 (Journal Identifier-Research Article-Article Number) and IT-2305-0112 (Journal Identifier-YearMonth-Article Number). Special issues may have their own codes that help to identify their manuscripts. Each time the manuscript is revised by the authors, a suffix of the form Rx can be added, where x is the number of the revision. Thus RA1234.R5 is the fifth revision of manuscript RA1234. The article numbers are generally assigned in sequence, not randomly. All communications regarding a particular manuscript should mention the identification number as this is the only unique marker for an individual manuscript and so greatly facilitates administration. If manuscripts are being submitted to a special issue, then the EA needs to ensure that authors can select the correct manuscript type, i.e. the name of the special issue has to be visible in the MMS to the submitting authors. When the deadline for the special issue has passed, the EinC should remind the EA to close off submissions (it may be done automatically) and if necessary to inform late authors that they have missed the deadline. These late authors can submit their manuscripts as regular (not special issue) manuscripts if they wish, and the EA can help to achieve this outcome.

After the EA has completed initial screening, the manuscript is assigned to the EinC, the EinC undertakes a further screening and if appropriate assigns the manuscript to an SE and the review process starts. At this point, the EA is no longer involved, though the EA will need to process any revised versions of the manuscript that are submitted before a final decision (Accept or Reject) is reached. If a manuscript is rejected, this is communicated directly to the authors by the EinC and a copy is sent to both the reviewers and the EA. If a manuscript is accepted, this is communicated directly to the authors by the EinC, with a copy to the EA and the Production Office (PO).

The PO, which is also often outsourced (in the Philippines for the journals I edit), has many staff members of whom one in particular, the Production Manager (PM), communicates regularly with the EinC. The PM is responsible for working with other staff, such as a copyediting team, a copyright permissions team, and a typesetting team, to prepare the accepted manuscript for publication. These people may be located in the PO or may be outsourced elsewhere, but the EinC generally does not need to be concerned with these internal processes, unless authors complain about poor quality of typesetting and the introduction of errors into accepted article proofs. However, the EinC does need to communicate with the PM to arrange which articles will be published in each issue of the journal. The PM may confirm the line-up of articles with a formal 'cover page' a few days before the issue goes to press (in the case of print journals) or is published online. Since the PM needs time to prepare each issue, it is sensible for the EinC to give at least a month's advance notice of which articles will be in the next issue. Towards the end of a calendar year, the publisher sends me a file with details of publication dates for each issue in the following year. This file includes the date by when all articles to be included in an issue need to be 'ready', i.e. have completed all formatting and typesetting requirements, and are 'assigned' to the issue.

At some journals, the EinC is not involved in selecting articles for issues and the PM handles this. In other journals, there are no issues at all, with articles published in a continuous stream as they become available. However, special issue articles may still be held back until all the accepted articles in the special issue are available, so that they can be released as a group. Many journals now operate 'early view' mechanisms, whereby accepted articles that are not yet assigned to an issue are made available on the journal's website where they can be seen, downloaded and of course cited by readers.

In commercially published journals, the publisher generally contracts all work to the EinC with the support of various EO and PO staff. In professional society-owned journals, there may be an additional layer of a publication committee within the professional society that engages (interferes) to a greater or lesser extent with both day-to-day operations and strategic or policy matters. However, queries may arise from time to time that require involvement of the publisher or the publication committee.

Thus, each EinC engages with a PM who is able to answer questions, resolve problems and also escalate matters to higher levels of production management if necessary. For instance, when a new special issue is commissioned, relevant information about the special issue needs to be made available on the journal's website, which is generally controlled by the publisher. Authors need to be able to select this special issue from a list of special issues in the MMS; this too requires the involvement of the publisher, since the EinC's permissions generally do not include this level of content management access. Occasionally, the MMS may have software bugs that need to be corrected. These situations require the involvement of the publisher, as well as technical support staff who are far beyond the reach of the EinC. The EinC may wish to update the journal's website from time to time, for instance so as to include new or revised guidelines for authors, reviewers, editors, special issues, manuscript types, or to reflect the changing composition of the editorial board as new SEs and AEs are appointed, or as SEs and AEs step down, change their affiliation or email address, etc. All of these updates need to be communicated to, approved by and later enacted by the publisher and its staff, as well as the publication committee where appropriate. Ideally these updates follow a routine process and can be effected within days, but I am aware of premier journals in my own field where the publisher's office is so short-staffed (or perhaps accords these revisions such a low priority) that the updates may require 6 months or even longer. This is a particularly frustrating situation for the EinC who has no power or authority to effect the changes directly, cannot compel anyone else to do so, cannot assign resources to the task and cannot terminate the employment of any employee in the production or publisher office, no matter how great their incompetence or indolence. The reputation of the journal can be damaged by this kind of negligence and the publisher only has itself to blame, yet the EinC, as the public face of the journal, is often the scapegoat. Fortunately, I have not had this experience since the publisher of the journals I edit is always prompt to take actions based on my requests, but I have witnessed the acute embarrassment of other less fortunate EinCs who can only apologise for a situation utterly beyond their control.

Publishers may produce an annual report in which they document key statistics of the journal, such as downloads, location of authors, the number of accepted articles, the locations of readers, the IF and other measures. For instance, a few years ago my publisher told me that China had become the third most significant location for downloads of articles from the journal, yet that few Chinese authors had had their articles accepted for publication and there were few Chinese scholars working for the journal as SEs or AEs. Although I was not specifically instructed to increase the number of accepted articles by Chinese authors or to increase their visibility in the editorial board, the discrepancy was noteworthy in itself. These aspects of diversity are tricky to handle and the EinC must tread cautiously. All submitted manuscripts are critically reviewed, but could there be a correlation between the ethnicity of the reviewers, the authors and the decision (Reject or Accept)? Put another way, are reviewers (or SEs or AEs) of one ethnicity or nationality more likely to accept manuscripts whose authors are of the same ethnicity or nationality? Similar questions could be raised about gender, epistemology, analytical techniques, etc.

I had no data to answer such a question and I don't think that the publisher did either, in large part because we do not collect metadata related to ethnicity and nationality, though it might be inferred from names and institutions, as well as a more careful review of personal websites. I feel that the question is a legitimate one, but it raises thorny issues that may be distinctly uncomfortable for a wide range of stakeholders: the discipline, the publisher, the EinC as well as anyone associated with the peer review process. However, publishers are at liberty to highlight these kinds of issues and expect that there will be some kind of coherent reaction from the EinC. My personal feeling is that there is no significant correlation at all: that all research is assessed entirely on its own merits and that manuscripts are accepted or rejected accordingly. However, I have noted earlier that reviewers can be biased, for example for or against particular methods or topics. Also, journals do have their own niches and it is conceivable that authors from one demographic segment tend to undertake research of a type that a particular journal generally does not publish.

The publisher's report can also be requested by the EinC in advance of an editorial board meeting, which is an appropriate venue for presentation and discussion of the key issues, including the example that I indicate above. Since all the information in the report is retrieved either from the MMS, the journal's website or from the publisher's own resources, the EinC should feel free to request any and all relevant information to be included in the report, though not necessarily for public consumption.

EinCs of journals that are commercially owned and published must also be concerned with the commercial side of their role: publishers have expectations for how journals should perform and implicitly how much revenue they generate. Publishers are also in competition with each other, not only for titles but also for intellectual footprint, i.e. how much research they publish. Occasionally, I receive an email from a person who indicates an interest in buying one of the journals that I edit. Since I don't actually own the journals, I can't sell them, and I refer such speculative buyers to the publisher. Notwithstanding this acquisitive interest, publishers are also interested in the impact that the journal has in its market and may wish to see that market expanded. Publishers track the performance of journals on a number of criteria, notably the numbers of submissions, downloads, citations, acceptance and rejection rates.

From a commercial perspective, it is likely that a publisher prefers a higher acceptance rate, since this will translate into more articles published, greater intellectual footprint and hence more revenue, but a journal editor may see the merits of a lower acceptance rate since this may be seen to reflect positively on the reputation of the journal, and hence implicitly the quality of the articles published in it. The EinC needs to navigate these mutually exclusive positions, but EinCs are often constrained in their behaviour by clauses in their contract that specify how many articles should be published in a given year. This constraint is more likely to affect the EinCs of commercially-owned journals, given the financial incentives to publish more, and less likely to affect the EinCs of society-owned journals, which may place a higher premium on reputation. EinCs who repeatedly fail to meet a contractual requirement regarding publication volume may find that they are out of a job: their contract is likely to specify exit terms that can be imposed by either party with sufficient advance notification.

However, to sweeten the EinC's position, commercial publishers tend to be more generous in how they remunerate their EinCs. The exact amount of an honorarium tends to be a closely guarded (commercial) secret, though I imagine that the EinCs of journals with higher publication volumes will also be rewarded in proportion. The honorarium is not strictly a salary; instead, it is intended that the money be used to promote the journal, for instance by attending conferences. Other people associated with the journal, i.e. SEs and AEs, are rarely compensated financially. This can be a concern as they may feel that the often considerable time that they invest on journal matters is not sufficiently appreciated, and I am aware of instances where SEs and AEs have voluntarily stepped down in protest at this lack of compensation.

In practice there is a trade-off and tensions between editor and publisher are unlikely to surface unless: the number of accepted articles drops precipitously; or the number of articles expected to be accepted rises too high or fast for the EinC to be able to guarantee a proportional throughput of quality articles; or there are major disagreements about journal policy. These might relate to what kind of articles should be published, how many and at what rate of annual increase, and at what quality level. Disagreements could also impinge on strategic concerns, e.g. the publisher decides that the journal should only be offered in an open access model, even though the EinC considers this not to be viable.

In contrast to commercially-owned journals, society-owned journals and university-owned journals have different business models that may affect their expectations of how the EinC works and what the EinC's responsibilities are. Even where a journal is owned by a society or university, it still has to be published and a commercial publisher may fulfil this role, which complicates the work of the EinC as it creates another layer of reporting. A society may have its own publication committee, and a representative of that society on the editorial board, or vice versa. These additional layers of bureaucracy are likely to significantly complicate the EinCs life and work. For instance, the EinC may need to report to a publication committee of a professional society on a regular basis, may need to seek that committee's endorsement for any policy changes, and may equally have to accept any policy changes determined by that committee, irrespective of whether the EinC has been consulted or not. To a large extent, additional layers of bureaucracy will act to stifle the EinC's initiatives, compared with the comparatively more liberal regime likely at commercially-owned journals where the EinC has a free hand to determine how to achieve contracted deliverables.

Where promoting the journal is concerned, publishers have an active interest and often do a very good job. EinCs may turn to their personal social media accounts to promote their journals: LinkedIn, Facebook, WeChat and X could all offer suitable opportunities. Publishers and individual journal titles may also have social media accounts that can be leveraged. EinCs should reach out to the publisher's marketing teams for ideas. They can also arrange for free copies of their journal to be available at conferences, or a QR code may be included in the communication to conference attendees that grants limited-time free access.

I have already mentioned the early view mechanisms that publishers favour because they can enhance revenue while maintaining copyright control. The role of such intermediaries as ResearchGate and Academia are more controversial, given that articles distributed through them will not generate revenue, yet they are extremely popular with authors who are unconcerned with revenue issues but keen to promote their research. Publishers generally prohibit authors from freely sharing their articles on intermediaries, unless the articles are gold open access, which I discuss in the next chapter. Nevertheless, irrespective of how research is shared, both authors and publishers are likely to have an interest in the citations that may accrue to the shared articles.

While EinCs may be in post for a few years or many, at some stage the EinC will step down or pass away, voluntarily or otherwise. A serving EinC who wishes to step down may have the opportunity to nominate a successor. The successor could be a long-serving SE or could be appointed from the outside. A managed transition period, which could be as long as a year, where the incumbent shares all communications and decisions with the next EinC, is perhaps ideal, since this will help to ensure both a smooth transfer of responsibilities and of knowledge and culture. But even when no transition is planned, there is a need for knowledge transfer and thus there is an argument that in any journal it may be sensible to identify a shadow EinC who could take over at short notice should the requirement exist. This shadow EinC needs to be kept up to date with everything that pertains to the management of the journal, indeed everything that I have covered in this book.

In order to make my own life as EinC easier, but also potentially to simplify the transition to a new EinC when that day comes, I maintain a number of folders and files with up-to-date information about the current situation at the journals I edit. I provide a detailed account of these files in Appendix C. They include: a complete detailed list of all articles that have been accepted for publication since the start of my tenure as EinC; a complete archive (in PDF) of all articles ever published by the journal; a complete list of all manuscripts under review; calls for current and past special issues; details of special issue SEs and AEs; details of manuscripts submitted to special issues and their current decision status; a simple count of how many manuscripts each SE and AE is handling, updated on a monthly basis; contact details for all SEs, AEs and EAB members; a list of keywords for all SEs and AEs, which I use when assigning guidelines for various stakeholders: authors, reviewers, special issue proposers, etc.; and IFs of 20 journals in the discipline backdated to 2010.

9

Continuing and Emerging Challenges and a Call to Action

Abstract Chapter 9 deals with some of the more generic emerging challenges that journal editors may face, now or in the foreseeable future. These include how to handle predatory journals, plagiarising authors, the open access movement, Generative Artificial Intelligence and manuscript formats that go beyond text and graphics. Each of these is discussed carefully with pointers to opportunities and illustrative examples.

Journal editors constantly face a range of emerging issues, though not all of these are problematic. Some may be opportunities to create new value for our stakeholders, others may challenge our operating procedures, while there are always a few that do cause considerable trouble. Some issues flare up and disappear just as quickly, but others persist and become part of the routine. In recent years, attention-worthy topics have included the impact of predatory journals, the incidence of plagiarism and other unethical behaviours, the emergence of the open access movement and most recently, the soaring popularity of generative Artificial Intelligence (AI) tools like ChatGPT.

9.1 Predatory Journals

Elmore and Weston (2020, p. 607) characterise predatory journals as 'publications that claim to be legitimate scholarly journals, but misrepresent their publishing practices. Some common forms of predatory publishing practices include falsely claiming to provide peer review, hiding information about

Article Publication Charges (APCs), misrepresenting members of the journal's editorial board, and other violations of copyright or scholarly ethics'. Predatory journals often have names that are very similar or even identical to those of legitimate journals, for instance by prepending such words as 'international', 'global', 'regional' or 'internet' to an existing journal's name. They may also include the names of legitimate journals in their website metatags, with the objective of misdirecting search engine results in their quest for new authors and readers. Many predatory journals will publish an article without a peer review process so long as the author pays a fee. Quite often, the topics addressed by published articles in predatory journals are completely unrelated to the nominal topic area of the journal itself.

Within the last few months, an alarming situation developed where it appeared that a legitimate journal, the *Scandinavian Journal of Information Systems* (*SJIS*), was the target of a hijacking attempt by malicious outsiders (Müller and Sæbø 2024). This was not the kind of hijack that I described earlier, where a group of researchers attempt to take the journal in a new direction. Instead, this was a more blatant attack where a scam website was developed that purported to be the real website of the journal. Why would anyone want to do this? Primarily because unsuspecting researchers who chance upon, or are invited to visit, this scam website may be persuaded to pay for their article to be accepted. Who are the victims of this deception? Usually, they are inexperienced researchers, often from developing countries, who don't realise that the scam website is a scam. In this kind of situation, the real EinC of the journal needs to take action against the scam website and its operators. In the course of the investigation, it turned out that the scam website operators had successfully managed to change a link on the Scopus website, pointing prospective authors towards the scam website not the real website. In order to protect the reputation of the real *SJIS* and its authors, the EinC of *SJIS* then took action to identify the domain name owner, to alert Scopus, to inform professional associations and their members, and to inform PayPal, which had been involved in payments for the scam website. At the time of writing, the situation is ongoing and certainly not fully resolved. I can only imagine that the situation has been a major headache for the EinC and publisher, as well as a significant drain on time and energy. This is the kind of situation that EinCs dread and hope never happens to them, but it may, and so EinCs must be aware of the predatory journal environment.

Predatory journals are, despite their notoriety, successful. This success is driven in large part by the low acceptance rates at legitimate journals and the strong need for researchers to publish, a situation that is also known as the publish or perish conundrum. Editors, 'often receive entreating emails from authors who ask how much they need to pay to get their manuscript accepted, pointing out that if they don't get it published, they will lose their jobs'

(Davison and Nielsen 2020). Soon-to-graduate PhD students pen similar missives, explaining that in order to graduate, they must have an article accepted by a journal, and that their graduation date is only a few weeks or days later, so please can the EinC send the acceptance letter immediately! Sometimes private agencies get involved, suggesting that they can supply large numbers of manuscripts for immediate publication (i.e. without review) with a payment (to the EinC's personal bank account) in the order of €500 per manuscript accepted.

Notwithstanding their unsavoury reputation, some predatory journals try hard to be accepted as legitimate journals. If they are successful, they may attract more submissions and make more money. One way to achieve legitimacy is to get their work cited in the existing legitimate (non-predatory) journals. If their work is cited, then it may appear to be influential, and that can only help the journal. Some journals that might be considered predatory are already indexed by Scopus, Google Scholar and the Science and Social Science Citation Indices. Occasionally I come across submissions to the journals I edit that extensively reference journals that could be considered predatory. What should I do? Return the manuscript to the author and require that the references are changed? Inform the SE and AE and suggest that if the manuscript is given a Revise and Resubmit decision, then changing the references could be one of the required actions? Superficially these approaches might seem sensible, but they also infringe the author's academic freedom to write and cite what they like. EinCs have to deal with tricky situations like this on a recurring basis and may be faulted no matter what approach they take. My only reasonable advice here is to create a policy, disseminate it to all SEs and AEs, inform authors in the author guidelines, and then enforce it consistently. All journals have policies that govern how they operate and what kinds of articles they publish. An example of a policy statement here could be something like: 'We reserve the right to require authors to modify their text following review as a condition of publication. Failure to adhere to the changes requested in editorial communication decisions may lead to the rejection of your manuscript'. What I would not do is to name any particular predatory journals or publishers in a policy statement. Firstly, there are too many to name. Secondly, there is no need to invite attention from specific predatory journals. Thirdly, neither you nor your publisher wants to be sued for defamation, whether the case has merit or not.

9.2 Plagiarism

Plagiarism is by no means a new concern for editors. The act of plagiarism is likely as old as human history: we reap the benefits of others' work by copying, and often forget (or fail) to give credit where credit is due. Copying is an essential survival technique and saves considerable time and energy (Pagel 2012). Wheels do not need to be reinvented each time we need them. In academic research, we expect that scholars will cite their sources appropriately, so as to give credit to those whose ideas they borrow or develop. This is a fundamental aspect of research ethics and the vast majority of researchers uphold these standards. At the same time, we routinely subject all submitted manuscripts to a plagiarism check using iThenticate,[1] a software programme that compares the text in a manuscript with a database containing close to 90 million published journal articles. When I undertake the screening of a manuscript, the iThenticate results are always available and I can examine the text similarities in detail if I want to. I am particularly concerned by situations where similar text occurs in complete sentences and paragraphs, i.e. it appears that the authors have copied large chunks of material from other published sources without attribution of the source.

There can be innocent reasons for unattributed copying, but they need to be examined carefully. For instance, I sometimes find that the source material is a PhD thesis and that the author is submitting a manuscript that draws largely on that thesis. This is not a problem in principle because the author will retain the copyright of the thesis and most PhD theses are not widely distributed, so the issue of the same material being published twice does not arise. However, it is a problem if someone other than the author is using large chunks of material from the thesis. In a recent case, I found that the supervisor of the student who wrote the thesis submitted a single-authored manuscript that extensively copied (plagiarised) the thesis, yet did not acknowledge the student author at all. When I raised this issue with the submitting author (the supervisor), he apologised for his 'oversight' and requested to change the authorship of the manuscript! I assume that had I not noticed he wouldn't have bothered. He also requested that I assign the same manuscript to one specific SE who, on further checking, turned out to be the supervisor's own supervisor! Given such blatant violations of ethical principles, I rejected this submission, informed the PhD student whose work had been plagiarised, and noted the name of the author for future reference.

I feel that a robust response is needed in incidents involving plagiarism. We cannot acquiesce in its practice, or let its adherents imagine that they can get away with no more than a slap on the wrist, and so we need to take resolute action to combat it. Plagiarism is one of the scourges of academic life. Not only does it violate the rights of authors but it tarnishes the reputation of journals and their publishers. It may also lead to legal issues associated with copyright violation. When I come across manuscripts with high similarity scores, I check

---

[1] http://www.ithenticate.com

the nature of the situation carefully. If the author is being careless with citations and the situation is not too serious, I will offer a desk revise and resubmit, i.e. ask the author to include quotation marks where appropriate and not to misappropriate ideas. If the situation is more serious, with paragraphs of material essentially lifted from another source without attribution, not only do I desk reject the manuscript, but I will take further actions. I request the plagiarising author to explain the situation. I will inform the author whose material has been copied about the situation. If the plagiarising author apologises, no further action may be needed, but very often the plagiarising author does not reply to my questions. I will then attempt to contact the employer of the plagiarising author, usually at the level of a Provost or Vice President for Research or Pro-Vice Chancellor or Vice Rector for Administration. I explain the situation that has arisen, provide evidence, note my communications with the plagiarising author and then leave the matter for the employer to deal with. The penalties that might be imposed vary, but I am aware of two cases (though I was not involved in either) involving plagiarism that was investigated by a university. In one, the plagiariser was demoted, in the other his employment contract was terminated. Getting involved in such cases is deeply unpleasant but EinCs cannot shirk their responsibilities.

9.3 Open Access

Open Access (OA) is an arrangement whereby research articles are made available for free for readers to access. Each publisher creates OA policies independently. OA is generally paid for by the authors of the articles concerned via Article Publication Charges (APC). At prestigious journals, APCs may reach USD5000 per article or more. APCs also constitute the primary revenue source for predatory journals. There are various models of OA, including: gold OA, where all content is freely available on the publisher's website; green OA, where authors can self-archive a pre-print of their article on their own website; bronze OA, where the publisher makes some articles, e.g. editorials, available for free on its website; hybrid OA, where journals publish both gold OA and not-OA articles that are not freely downloadable but subject to purchase or subscription requirements; platinum or diamond OA, where all content is available for free on the publisher's website and there are no APCs. This last arrangement generally requires some other form of funding arrangement, e.g. a donor or advertising to cover costs. For the record, the two journals that I edit have a hybrid OA policy: authors can pay for gold OA if they want, but they can also publish closed-access articles that are only available to individuals who pay for access (either per article or via a personal subscription to a journal), or who have institutional access (e.g. via a university library); in addition, there is a bronze OA option for editorials, and a platinum OA option for readers located in less developed countries.[2]

When OA was first mooted it was thought to constitute a threat to commercial publishers since they would lose revenue if they could not charge for access. APCs for gold OA have mitigated that concern, i.e. transferring the costs from the readers to the authors, though there are now concerns that gold OA fees are too high. Some institutions and countries have negotiated transformative agreements that permit all researchers to submit their research without fees to a gold OA publication process. In some other countries, researchers supported by grants are mandated to submit their articles via a gold OA process, with the (predicted) APCs included in their research grant applications as part of their budget.

As an EinC, I feel that OA is primarily a matter between authors and the publisher. However, I have always supported a platinum OA policy for developing countries where most researchers' salaries are so low that gold OA fees are beyond their means and yet where it is essential that high-quality research content is available for free access. Nevertheless, I also see citation benefits associated with OA-publication. Published gold, bronze and platinum OA articles are often downloaded more frequently (because there are no charges to readers) and consequently tend to be also more highly cited. The publisher of the two journals I edit reports (based on data for all the journals it publishes) that OA articles outperform subscription (i.e. not OA) articles across many performance metrics, with 3.2 times more downloads and 1.5 times more citations. There is a dark side to OA. Junior scholars in particular may feel the obligation to pay for OA, even if they have no funds to draw on, if they feel that OA will lead to their articles being cited more and thus their reputation being burnished further. Such consequences might be associated with the increased likelihood of their contract being renewed. Indeed, predatory journals already cater to this market by offering to publish almost anything so long as the author pays.

Some journals are moving to gold OA publishing models (i.e. with no hybrid option) and I suspect that unfortunately this is the long-term trend. From the publisher's point of view, a gold OA process, coupled with transformative agreements, is much simpler to administer. However, I fear that such a move will have the effect of excluding authors whose research is not funded or who are not covered by transformative agreements. If authors have to pay their APCs from their pockets, this will be a significant disincentive to

---

[2] World Bank indicators are commonly used, e.g.: https://data.worldbank.org/country/XL

undertake and publish research that will disproportionately affect scholars in the less developed countries in particular, where resources to support research have historically been weaker.

9.4 Generative AI

The hot topic for the EinC since early 2023 has been the impact that generative AI tools like ChatGPT may have on the publication process. As EinC, I wrote some of my earlier thoughts on this emerging topic in Davison et al. (2023b). Some pundits believe that even though the technology is still at a nascent stage, it will soon be possible for authors to commission an AI programme to create a complete research manuscript. This will doubtless raise ethical issues about provenance and who should be entitled to claim authorship. The prospect of large numbers of such AI-generated manuscripts being submitted concerns editors who will have to reach decisions, a time-taking process. Meanwhile, I understand that the publishers may screen submitted manuscripts to check if they are AI-authored. Editors need to work together with publishers to develop policies about what is permissible where AI tools are concerned. It seems impractical to ban their use: there may be situations where AI tools offer a superlative level of analysis compared to human brains, able to see patterns that we cannot detect. Indeed, spell checking and grammar checking tools are already part of the mainstream, and some journals have authorised the use of AI tools for improving the quality of writing. Dwivedi et al. (2023), a consortium of some 73 authors, provide an extensive set of commentaries about ChatGPT and its potential impacts across a multitude of domains. However, this is a dynamic space and I can only expect that by the time this book is published, the AI scene will have evolved in ways I cannot yet imagine, rendering much of this text obsolete or of no more than passing historical value. Nevertheless, academic research articles that focus on generative AI are starting to emerge and I anticipate that this will constitute a cornucopia of research opportunities for some time to come.

9.5 Beyond Text: Presentation Opportunities

Traditionally, academic journals have limited themselves to manuscripts that are largely comprised of text, supplemented with figures and tables. In the last few years, the opportunity for authors to make other material available has arisen. For instance, when an article is accepted for publication, authors are invited to provide links to their research data, code, or other materials that may be located in dedicated research repositories. They can also upload a video that captures the essence of their research. In my experience few authors take advantage of this opportunity, but generative AI might have a role to play. Gaskin et al. (2016) outline how authors could leverage multimedia in the dissemination of their research findings, essentially rendering a summary of the article in a format that is perhaps more easily digestible by practitioners in particular, but also all readers who are more attuned to a visual presentation of material. Multimedia can also serve to increase the interaction between authors and their readers. This may be salient for topics like information security, where there is an intended andragogical effect: the authors hope not only to inform readers about the phenomenon, but also to help them develop their own knowledge through an interactive experience that could be tailored to the needs to different readers (novices, experts; students, practitioners, professors; speakers of different languages). A heightened degree of interactivity may also benefit the journal, especially if it wishes to explore or develop new reader markets. For instance, Gaskin et al. (2016) describe what they term 'Narrative Animated Videos' (NAV) that could be created with generative AI if authors feel that they don't have the skills (or interest) to do so themselves. Alternatives to the NAV are podcasts and graphical abstracts: the latter in particular may be amenable to interpretation with generative AI. Generative AI-based interpretations may be of particular value to practitioner readers who are not familiar with academic jargon, yet see the potential value in academic research.

9.6 Scanning for the Future

EinCs have a responsibility to scan the horizon for new trends, tools, techniques and threats. Open science and research transparency are two such trends, each of which may affect the peer review process (Wolfram et al. 2020). Some trends will be long in the making and may be visible long before they create the opportunity or threat that needs to be leveraged or countered. Others may appear without warning. Howsoever the case, the EinC, informed or assisted by a broad network of contacts, has the strategic prerogative to ensure the continued thriving of the journal. Although much of the EinC's work may seem routine, even mundane, a constant suspicion and alertness to the environment is healthy. EinCs need to plan for the future, an idea that I will return to in the next chapter.

10

Theorising Editing

Abstract In this closing chapter, I attempt to develop what amounts to a theory of editing. I try to see the world of the editor through the eyes of an anthropologist, to narrate what it is that editors do, and to examine the strategic opportunities that arise. By drawing on my own prior research, i.e. over the last quarter of a century, I formulate a descriptive theory of the world of the editor. I also illustrate this theory with data from my own experience, but observe that this can only be my own experience: each editor needs to apply the theory individually and uniquely. Indeed, they may also feel the need to modify the theory itself.

In the course of writing this book, I shared early drafts with friends and colleagues who have provided extensive commentary.[1] A person to whom I want to draw special attention now is Allen Lee. Although Allen has retired from formal academic life, he is still active in the community and, importantly from my perspective, is the former editor of one of our premier journals, *MIS Quarterly*. Allen made a suggestion that led to my writing this chapter. It was not part of my original design for the book, so I thank Allen for stimulating my thinking with his trenchant remarks. I quote from his original feedback:

> Right now, your book is, as expected, atheoretical. In fact, it is exemplary as … a "practitioner book", where scholars are the practitioners. Well, you have the freedom to add a chapter that introduces theory to your perspective on the art

[1] See acknowledgements

of journal editing. What theory might be introduced? ... I see you as having a theory-rich background. Surely, some/much of it has application to the art of journal editing. In short, the book you've written so far takes the perspective of a native. The additional chapter I'm asking you to write would be from the perspective of an anthropologist or other social scientist.

Mulling over this idea, I was attracted by the notion of both theorising the art of journal editing, and of taking an anthropological stance in the writing of it. In essence, the challenge is to use my understanding of both journal editing and theory writing to write a story about journal editing as an insider (I can't escape my role or eliminate my prior knowledge) that leads to a theory consumable by both outsiders (the audience who are not currently journal editors) and other insiders (people who are current journal editors).

Why a story? Stories are an essential device for the anthropologist. Anthropologists are interested in how stories help people to make sense of their lives, and they tell stories in order to share their own sensemaking about others' lives. Theoretical storytelling is a way to approach theory through the medium of a story in which the various actors in the story engage in sensemaking. In this chapter, my story relates to the genre of journal editing and in particular the work of the EinC. For the most part, there is only one stakeholder, me, though I do refer to a few other people as well. By telling a story about my experiences as an EinC, I hope to provide an anthropological account that helps both me and you to make sense of my experiences. I will interweave theories and theoretical ideas as I tell the story and then I will craft a new theory out of this theoretical story. How will this theoretical story differ from the previous nine chapters? Well, as Allen Lee remarked, the first nine chapters are both atheoretical and essentially practical. In them I describe many aspects of the work that EinCs do, but in an atheoretical way. Now, in this closing chapter, I will retell the story of what it is that EinCs do, through the lens of how one particular EinC thinks about what he does and why he does it. In retelling the story, in admittedly a much-compressed form, I will deliberately bring theoretical ideas into the narrative as a spur to my sensemaking. The story will include reflections about the story, and the theory. Towards the end of the chapter, I will aim to bring together the various strands of the story into a single theoretical narrative, i.e. a theory of 'the humble art of journal editing'. The nature of a story is to be a little less tight than formal academic writing, so you may detect stylistic changes in this chapter. These are deliberate.

What kind of theory building process should I follow? The literature is replete with treatises about what theory is or isn't, and what it consists of.

Theory itself remains a polyseme, meaning different things to different people. For my purposes, I will define a theory as a way of making sense of the world, in this case the world of the EinC. I also think that my theory should be able (following Dubin 1978) to explain both *what* an EinC may do, and *how* and *why* the EinC may do it. Theories are commonly expected to provide 'a coherent description, explanation and representation of observed or experienced phenomena' (Gioia and Pitre 1990, p. 587). Some theories explain situations, others describe cause and effect relationships (Gregor 2006). The theory that I propose to develop here is an explanatory theory, tracing the activities and thoughts of the EinC and explaining why they are the way they are. I share Lewin's (1945) assertion that a good theory will be practical, balancing comprehensiveness with parsimony (Dubin 1978) and be both 'plausible ... and correspondent with presumed realities' (Weick 1989). I want my theory to be grounded in the world of the EinC, and as such it should be practical and plausible. Although the vast majority of researchers apply or develop theory, there are remarkably few articles that describe in detail how to develop theory. In prior work, my colleagues and I have developed an instrumental theory of how to build theory (Martinsons et al. 2015) that also informs my account here.

My 'data' is limited to my own experiences, which are highly subjective since I don't plan to interview or observe other editors, though I will ask them for feedback. An inductive approach is possible, and would be consistent with much of my own prior theoretical work. But there is also merit in a deductive approach: this would allow me to develop theory from my own prior work, and that of others. Indeed, this is what Allen alluded to this when he referred to my rich theoretical background, suggesting that I may be able to interweave some of my prior theoretical work into a new theory of journal editing. A third approach is the abductive, which Díaz Andrade (2023) figuratively characterises as a dance between theory and data. He asserts that 'The information systems researcher equipped with a robust understanding of relevant theories and endowed with an inquisitive mind open to exploring unusual observations can capitalise on what abductive thinking affords to make sense theoretically of empirical evidence creatively' (ibid., p. 275). A key element of abductive reasoning that seems to me to be very appropriate is the principle of abductive inference, which, in contrast to deductive (what must be) and inductive (what actually is) reasoning, incorporates the notion of what may be, i.e. a 'satisficing explanation for a specific consequence' (Lee et al. 2011, p. 4). As I will explain more carefully later, it is not my intention that my theory of the world of the EinC be deterministic (what EinCs must do) or be limited to my own experience (what I do) but instead be a representation of the possibilities, the things that EinCs may do.

My starting point for this process was to read the previous nine chapters again, so as to ensure that I had most of the relevant facts in active memory, and to briefly review in my mind some of the theory articles that Allen suggested, as well as a few others, and see where those theories might inform what it is that EinCs may do. These articles involve theoretical discussions about: guanxi (Ou et al. 2014), personal and cultural factors (Huang et al. 2008), culture and the way it complicates interactions (Davison 2002), strategic decision-making (Martinsons and Davison 2007), informal knowledge sharing (Davison et al. 2013), and global virtual teams (Hardin et al. 2007). To these, I will append further articles in which I engaged in theoretical discussions about: workarounds that employees create when corporate systems prove inadequate (Davison et al. 2021); the organisational citizenship that is manifested when employees do more than is expected of them (Davison et al. 2020); and the way technology both interrupts people and enables them to interact with each other (Ou and Davison 2011). Finally, I mention the Balanced Scorecard (Martinsons et al. 1999), an instrumental theory that is valuable in strategic planning and that I will use to frame the emerging theory.

I don't plan for this chapter to be anything like a traditional research article. Indeed, it functions more as a conclusion to this book than as anything else. Beyond Allen's recommendation, the motive for writing the chapter is to craft a simple way of explaining the possibilities of the what, how and why of EinC behaviours. If there is an introduction, then it is the preceding nine chapters. There is relevant literature, some of it mentioned above, but I will come to it as I need it. Will there be a peer review process? Not in the normal sense of the expression, but yes, I will ask my peers (Allen in particular) to review this chapter as they review the other chapters, and to offer feedback. This is not a blind review process, since I know who I am inviting to review and they know who I am. As far as possible, the writing style in this chapter will resemble the stream of consciousness style that has largely informed the previous nine chapters, but, as befits a story, it will also be a little less tight.

10.1 Background

What is it that EinCs do? Fundamentally, they do one thing: they manage a review process for individual manuscripts, in order to curate content that makes a contribution to knowledge and is thus worthy of publication. In order to achieve this outcome, there are many subsidiary activities that they perform. These include building and sustaining relationships with a large number of people who may be authors, reviewers, readers, publishers, or someone else. They create a culture around the review process that to some degree regulates the behaviour of the different people associated with research publication. They formulate a position for the journal that sets it up for success, and hopefully a renowned reputation, now and in the future. These are the higher-level activities in which they engage, and some EinCs may view these as their primary occupational focus. But in order to achieve these outcomes, EinCs need to develop a certain skill set. The practice of these skills is something that an external observer might be able to see and measure, and that's where the anthropologist comes in.

Let me digress a little with a venture into two anthropologists' minds.

Ingold (2013, p. 1), in a remarkable and slim tome titled '*Making: Anthropology, Archaeology, Art and Architecture*', narrates how, when living among the Saami in northern Finland, his requests for information about how to undertake practical tasks were often met with the terse 'Know for yourself!' He continues (ibid.): 'But after a while I realised that ... they wanted me to understand that the only way one can really know things – that is, from the very inside of one's being – is through a process of self-discovery. To know things, you have to grow into them, and let them grow in you, so that they become a part of who you are. Had my companions offered formal instruction by explaining what to do, I would have had only the pretence of knowing, as I would find out the moment I tried to do as I was told. The mere provision of information holds no guarantee of knowledge, let alone of understanding'.

Descola (1996), in his seminal and much more hefty volume '*The Spears of Twilight: Life and Death in the Amazonian Jungle*', discusses how he informed his own supervisor, the French structural anthropologist Claude Levi-Strauss about his intended plans for ethnographic field research among the Shuar of Ecuador, and asked for feedback. The response was that he should 'follow the lie of the land' rather than expecting to stick to pre-determined techniques and styles of enquiry.

Both Ingold and Descola tell me that learning takes place in context, where the learner adapts to the infinite variety of circumstances as they unfold. One learns by experiencing situations and letting those situations grow on you so that they become part of you. This seems to me to be an insightful and accurate portrayal of how it is that EinCs learn. Given the infinite variety of circumstances, learning and knowledge acquisition is a life-long process, and this should be no less true for the EinC, yet most EinCs have tenures of a few years at best. It doesn't seem long enough to accumulate and learn from more than a handful of the experiences. Meanwhile, when the EinC steps down the knowledge is largely retained by the now former EinC, not transferred to the new EinC. This also provides a motive for me to write this book and tell this story: I hope that some of what I learned will be accessible to others who can more readily assimilate the knowledge and recontextualise it for their own purposes.

Thus, to a significant degree, the purpose of this book is to reveal what I know about what it is that EinCs do, how they do it, how they prepare for it, and what skills they need to do it well. I realise that there are different types of both journal (some are elite, others are not; some are broad, others are niche; some are commercially owned, others are society owned) and editor (some are newly appointed whereas others are very experienced in their roles). I can't speak to each of these possible combinations individually, but I hope that there is a take-away message for each type of editor in each type of journal, a message that can be adapted to their individual and idiosyncratic circumstances, just as my own account is also individual and idiosyncratic.

There is also a chance that my story may count for little more than an armchair account of the EinC's life, akin to a coffee-table account of life among the Saami or the Shuar, unless you, the reader, try to put some of these ideas into action. There is nothing wrong with coffee-table books, and as the author I (promise that I) won't be unhappy if that's what happens to this book, though the lack of glossy pictures may preclude that fate; relegation to a distant bookshelf seems more likely. But I hope that for some readers, this book will be a spur to action, to engage in a process of self-discovery and thus to 'know for yourselves'.

What would the anthropologist make of EinCs? No doubt the anthropologist would engage in a careful and extended observation of what it is that EinCs do, engage them in conversation, and attempt as far as possible to get inside their minds. To do this directly is, of course, problematic unless you can persuade the EinC to allow him/herself to be wired up to a CAT or MRI scan on a regular basis (Owen 2017) at the same time as the EinC is engaged in journal-focused tasks. But if the anthropologist is also an EinC, then perhaps there is the chance of a confessional ethnographic account. I don't pretend to be an expert anthropologist or ethnographer, but there is no time like the present to start.

How to tell this story? I decided to take as a starting point the account of a knowledge worker, since EinCs are also knowledge workers, called Bob, who is the central protagonist of Halverson's (2004) story.

10.2 The Editor-in-Chief's Story

Every morning, when I turn on my computer and check the 100 or so emails, I will see messages that pertain to my EinC role. Some are from authors, some from SEs and AEs, and others from the EA advising me that newly submitted manuscripts need screening or reviewed manuscripts need a decision. During the course of a 24-h day, I suppose that on average there are 15–20 such communications. The quotidian processing of these emails, like many others, is not unduly onerous, but there is method and theory here. There is a way to make sense of what I do.

The EinC's world is largely a virtual world. I have never met the EA or PM, or the vast majority of the authors who submit or the reviewers who review. I have met all the SEs and the vast majority of AEs (the exception being a few of the most newly appointed), though I don't meet them very often. In this virtual world, I depend on various technologies to undertake my tasks. Email is the most important communication tool. I might promote the journal on LinkedIn once in a while, but otherwise I abjure social media. I can't imagine using WhatsApp, WeChat, X or a similar messaging tool to contact any of the journal's stakeholders, though that's not to say that it can't be done; I know that some other EinCs are much more social-media active than I am. I do use Skype, MS Teams and Zoom occasionally if there is a need for a more direct communication, though I seldom turn on my camera, so it is little more than VoIP. But email is one technology that I can't do without. I first used email in 1986 and it has not changed a great deal since then. The other technology that is critical is the MMS. Manuscript Central is one of the better-known MMS, but there are others. The MMS incorporates a wide variety of functions that are critical to various parts of the submission and review process. The exact instantiation of the MMS varies from journal to journal. Some have more functionality than others, some are easier to use than others, and some are downright awkward. I'll come to some problems that I experience with the MMS that I use, and the way that I deal with those problems, later.

In my virtual world, I interact through email with hundreds of individual people individually, and thousands more via Listservs. Over the course of my life as a researcher in general, and of my tenure as EinC in particular, I have developed my own transactive memory network (Jarvenpaa and Majchrzak 2008) of experts, such that I know who is the best person to help me with a task. In the context of a journal, the network is smaller because it is limited to the SEs and AEs who work there, perhaps 100 people, but still, I know who knows the answer to a specific question, and I know who has the skills to handle a particular manuscript. I could also say that I know who will reject a manuscript and who will give the authors a second chance. I know who will complete the screening in 24 h (or less) and who may need a week. I know who will write a decisive but rather abrupt three-line review and who will write three pages of graceful, flowing prose. This knowledge about people is invaluable for me in my EinC role. But my meta knowledge, which I am describing here, is not the same as the detailed knowledge, the characteristics of the individual people. I am not going to tell you who these people are, and arguably you don't need to know for the purpose of the theory. You can know for yourself if you wish via your own transactive memory networks.

When I am thinking about which SE to assign to a manuscript, it is not just a matter of the skill set. It may be that five SEs are more or less equally qualified. Some may currently be handling more manuscripts than others and I don't want to overload people. Some might be requested by the author, so I need to consider if there is a conflict of interest. An SE approached me with this kind of question recently and said 'I don't know why the AE asked me to reassign the manuscript to a different AE. Is there a conflict of interest with the author?'. I looked at the MMS, found the manuscript in question, and then understood: I recalled that the author had completed her PhD in the same institution where the AE now worked (even though they now work in different places) and so yes, the AE would probably know the author rather too well.

But it's more than just these simple coincidences. I have a principle that I try to ensure that there is diversity in review teams, such that while the review team should be variously familiar or expert with the topic, method, epistemology, I prefer that they do not all come from the same country, let alone institution. Thus, if a manuscript is submitted from authors based at the University of British Columbia in Vancouver, Canada, I would prefer that between the SE, AE and two reviewers there are people from both the same and from different continents/countries. A Canadian perspective may be very valid, but four Canadian perspectives seems a bit too much. I'd like to complement the Canadian perspective with one from China or Israel or Nigeria or Latvia. Of course, this is not always possible, but I would certainly try to avoid the situation where the entire review team comes from one country. This is easier said than done, since not all AEs (who typically have the responsibility to identify reviewers) have sufficiently diverse networks beyond their own country and it is easier for them to recruit reviewers from within their one-country network. This is why I like the both SE and myself to be involved in reviewer assignments. It helps to avoid unintentional conflicts of interest. It may sometimes lead to cultural complications: people from different cultures naturally tend to have different ways of looking at and explaining the world. The AE's life is made harder when the AE needs to reconcile or at least respect the disparate views of culturally diverse reviewers. But authors need to remember that they are writing for a global audience, and a culturally diverse review team can help the author to strengthen the presentation such that it is accessible by a diverse audience.

A culturally diverse review team can also dilute the cultural biases that might exist in a more culturally monolithic review team. When I refer to culture here, I am not only thinking of societal culture (e.g. at the country level), but also methodological and epistemological culture. Recently, I encountered a situation (not at one of the journals I edit) where a manuscript that used an ethnographic approach was assigned to an AE who knew nothing of ethnography; this AE assigned the manuscript to two reviewers who knew nothing of ethnography either! The result was sadly predictable: rejection without any real appreciation of the merits of the research itself, only the rather dismissive remark from one reviewer: 'I don't like ethnography as a method. Why don't you do empirical work and collect survey data?'. Alas, the AE did not take issue with this patently incorrect and blatantly solipsistic remark. For instance, the AE could have rescinded the review or even intervened by offering a more generous assessment of the manuscript. When the author complained to the EinC, no response was forthcoming, despite repeated reminders. As an EinC myself I was appalled. I hope that not only I but also the SEs and AEs at the journals I edit never think or behave like this. If none of the review team is culturally or methodologically familiar with the research that they reviewing, the manuscript in question may have little chance of surviving the review process. I suggest that a more methodologically and culturally diverse review team could have delivered a very different outcome.

It often happens that reviewers are late. Sometimes, alas, SEs and AEs are also late. By 'late' I primarily mean alive but delayed in delivering their review or report, but occasionally 'late' means 'passed away'. When this happens, and when there appears to be little prospect that the individual is going to deliver the review or report any time soon, I feel the need to intervene. If a reviewer is significantly late, then we may need to assign a new reviewer who can guarantee to deliver quickly. Such reviewers do exist, but the EinC may need to ask them personally. EAB members constitute one category of emergency reviewer. Personal contacts are another. Very often, they can guarantee a high-quality review in a week or less, which is most helpful. If the AE or SE is late and unresponsive then a new AE or SE must be found quickly. In general, the SE or AE may need to step down unless there is an extremely good justification for the delay. Finding a new AE or SE is not impossible, but requires some juggling as some are better at this kind of sudden assignment handling than others. That said, there are others who seem to relish it and as such are extremely helpful. This latter behaviour corresponds to what is known in the literature as organisational citizenship behaviour (OCB) (Organ 1988), which involves doing more than your job description says you should do, often out of a sense of greater loyalty or responsibility to the organisation. In an earlier chapter, I explained how I see the journal as a family. SEs and AEs who subscribe to this notion of a family are as a rule very willing to enact the OCB that I describe above.

To continue the implications of the family metaphor, I strongly encourage the sharing of experiences and knowledge among family members. I do not want AEs in particular to feel that they are on their own when it comes to recruiting reviewers or making a recommendation. Instead, we have a vibrant support network of SEs and where necessary EAB members, as well as the EinC, to support them in different ways. Some of that sharing takes place through email, but some also at our occasional editorial board meetings. When I meet SEs and AEs, I often invite them to lunch or dinner as a way of demonstrating my sincere appreciation of their time and energy invested in the journal. I encourage them to share experiences and am more than willing to offer advice if it is sought. Another channel of support is the editorials that I write for each regular issue (special issues have their own editorials written by the guest editors). These editorials are written for a variety of stakeholders: potential authors and reviewers, but also current AEs and SEs. For instance, the July 2023 editorial related to the expectations for a theoretical contribution that we have at the *ISJ*, and indeed the different expectations for different genres of research. I anticipate that this editorial may provide valuable support to SEs and AEs who want to encourage authors to focus on their theoretical contribution, or perhaps to admonish authors for failing to do so. An editorial like this draws a line for the journal and establishes an expectation. I expect that SEs and AEs will also share knowledge with each other without my involvement, for instance when communicating about how to handle the review of a particular manuscript. I see this as an apprenticeship model where the SEs both guide the review process and provide support to the AE, working together. Since the SE and AE are unlikely to be collocated, they too form a virtual team (albeit of two people) who need to find a way to work together across time and space.

A characteristic of Chinese society is the sociocultural phenomenon known as 'guanxi'. Although guanxi can be translated simply (and simplistically) as 'relationship', my preferred translation is also an explanation: Guanxi is manifested as a multiplicity of 'social ties that are created and maintained between firms and individuals, that are founded on shared interests and benefits' (Davison et al. 2023a). I regard guanxi as a meta construct because it 'has many sub-components including: obligation (to help people with whom you have guanxi); favours (that you give to and receive from people with whom you have guanxi); reciprocity (because you need to behave reciprocally with the people with whom you have guanxi); affection or care (for the people with whom you have guanxi); status (with your guanxi partners); and trust (in and from the people with whom you have guanxi)' (Davison et al. 2023a). Guanxi-type relationships tend to be strong, deep and long-lasting. They are often invaluable to the EinC who can call on them for help in a variety of circumstances, so long as the EinC recognises that others may call on them for help as well.

There is of course a danger here, a dark side, because guanxi is also associated with corruption, or the expectation of favours where none are due or where they cannot be given. Thus, if an author with whom I have strong guanxi expects that I will accept his manuscript, irrespective of its quality, that can create a problem. If the result of the review process is not favourable and a rejection is necessary, what happens? Will the individual lash out and accuse me of not honouring the guanxi? Will the individual ostracise me and denigrate me to his network? Will I worry about this? The EinC cannot prevent an author from submitting a manuscript on the basis that the author and EinC have a conflict of interest. An established EinC may have hundreds or thousands of contacts: are all these people barred from submitting their work to the journal? In practice, therefore, a measure of common sense must apply to both authors and EinCs. The primary responsibility of the EinC is to manage the review process with integrity. Conflicts of interest cannot be entirely excluded, yet the EinC cannot recuse himself every time, so the EinC will have to make tough decisions on occasion. Authors need to respect this as being part of the way the research and publication process works. Speaking entirely for myself I have lost track of the number of times my own manuscripts have been rejected by fellow editors at our journals. It's entirely normal: the more you write, the more you will be rejected!

Exception management is thus likely to be a key part of the EinC's story. While, many activities are routine and regular, others are occasional and irregular. If they are serious, they can interrupt all other tasks until a solution is found. Exceptions have to be tackled with care because there is always the potential for them to cause harm, whether that is a loss of face for the editor or publisher, or something less dramatic. For instance, reviewers occasionally ask the AE for deadline extensions, but the AEs frequently fail to tell the SE and EinC, and also fail to update the MMS, so there is no record and no one else knows. This is problematic for all concerned. The EinC may write to the reviewers to remind them; the reviewer retorts that the AE has granted an extension, even though the AE has no authority to do so and has not told anyone else about the extension.

From time to time I have to deal with problems that are caused by the EO. I ask them to do something and they say that it can't be done. For instance, I ask them to arrange for an automatic email to be sent to the AE when a reviewer declines to do the review. They cannot comply because the MMS software cannot be customised in this way. I ask that when a manuscript is submitted to a special issue, it is pre-coded with a unique identifier for that special issue. Thus, if the special issue is called Enterprise Systems and I want all submissions to this special issue to be coded ES-xxxx, they say that it's not possible. Instead, they code all special issue manuscripts using the generic SIP-xxxx format. I explain that this is problematic because I have multiple special issues in progress simultaneously and I need to code the submissions separately, e.g. ES-xxxx, TQ-xxxx, DS-xxxx. They still say that it can't be done. Well, I know that it is possible because I can do it myself. I just have to access the submission data and change the code myself. It is not difficult and takes about 30 seconds to achieve for each manuscript, though there is no batch process available and each manuscript has to be modified individually. Is it my job to do so? Am I stepping on someone's toes or invading their space? Perhaps I am, but sometimes these kinds of stronger measures are necessary.

I have developed a lot of back office workaround solutions, my own private fixes and exception handling arrangements for problems that the EO cannot or doesn't want to do. If authors write in to say that they do not want to revise their manuscript and instead want to withdraw their manuscript, this is hard to achieve because there is no withdraw function. The EO normally says that we should wait for the expiry of the resubmit deadline, but the MMS will keep sending reminder messages to the authors. It's simpler to backdate the deadline for resubmission, to any date before today, and then the manuscript disappears from the active list (though it is still kept in the archive for another 2 years and could be resurrected if necessary) and the reminders stop. If a person requests to be removed from the MMS this is also difficult: I don't know of a direct way to remove an account. But I can merge two accounts together. If I merge an unwanted account with a dummy account that I have created for this purpose but that actually belongs to no one, the unwanted account disappears.

CUSTOMERS	PRODUCT/SERVICES
· Authors · Readers · Senior and Associate Editors · Reviewers · Proposers of Special Issues · Publication Office	· Reviews and Decisions · Communications with customers · Updates to the website · Editorials · Policies · Documents for journal management
MAJOR WORK PROCESSES AND ACTIVITIES **(Undertaken by the EinC)**	
Manuscript-Related Activities	Other Activities Related to the Journal
· Screen submitted manuscripts for suitability / fit with the journal · Assign suitable manuscripts to SEs for further checking and the review process · Work with SEs and AEs to identify suitable reviewers · Chase authors, reviewers, SEs and AEs who miss deadlines · Make and communicate decisions (Accept, Revise, Reject) following the screening & review of manuscripts · Inform the publication office about the line-up of accepted articles in each issue	· Create policies that guide authors, reviewers, SEs/AEs and other stakeholders · Make ad hoc decisions about people and processes as circumstances dictate · Write editorials for each regular issue · Promote the journal and each issue in different forums · Assess special issue proposals · Monitor the website and recommend updates · Monitor the journal's status with regard to readership, citations, reputation, quality · Evaluate feedback and respond to complaints from authors and other stakeholders · Maintain documentation (in Word or Excel) related to the journal and its SEs and AEs

PARTICIPANTS	INFORMATION	TECHNOLOGIES
· The Editor in Chief	· Submitted (under review) manuscripts · Meta data describing manuscripts and their authors · Details of SE and AE expertise, workloads · Transactive memory of who (SEs and AEs) knows what or is an expert in which areas · Accepted manuscripts · Proposals for special issues	· MMS · Email · Social Media · Journal website and e-library · Office Applications (Word and Excel)

Fig. 10.1 A work systems snapshot for the regular work done by the EinC

In thinking about all these activities, routine and exceptional, I realised that Alter's (2013) Work Systems Snapshot (WSS), an integral part of the Work Systems Method, provides a simple way of capturing the essence of what it is that EinCs do. The WSS that I show below (see Fig. 10.1) highlights the key components of the work that is done by the EinC. Although the components of Fig. 10.1 do not themselves comprise a theory, being merely a list of activities, they nevertheless contribute to the theorising process. The structure of a WSS is simple but effective because it forces the author to consider carefully exactly what kind of work is being done. There is only one *participant* in the current analysis because I am focusing exclusively on the work done by the EinC. The *information* box contains all the information sources that the EinC needs to complete work. Most of the information items are documents or files with information. However, the exception is the 'transactive memory' of the EinC, i.e. the knowledge of the attributes of (primarily) the different SEs and AEs who work for the journal. The *technology* box should include all the technologies that the EinC uses on a regular basis. The central part of the WSS illustrates the *major work processes and activities* undertaken by the EinC. I have not listed all possible work processes and activities as the list could be very long, but those indicated here are the major ones that EinCs are likely to spend most time on. Some of them relate to daily work, such as manuscript processing tasks. Others are more occasional, involving special issues, communications with the publication office, editorials, etc. However, the rare activities such as dealing with plagiarising authors or unethical reviewers are not listed here. The *customers* are the people or entities who receive a *product or service* from the Work System. Customers can be internal or external, and therefore the products and services include items suitable for each audience. Although the WSS is helpful in outlining the regular work activities of the EinC, some aspects of the EinC's work are missing, most notably strategic plans and the culture and reputation that the EinC crafts. I turn to the strategic perspective next.

10.3 A Strategic Perspective on Editing

At the end of the previous chapter, I indicated that EinCs need to make plans for the future in order to ensure the continued relevance and viability of the journal for a variety of stakeholders. A tool which can be applied to such a planning endeavour is the Balanced Scorecard (BSC). The BSC was first developed in the 1990s (Kaplan and Norton 1992) as a way of demonstrating how future value could be created within organisations. A conventional BSC has four perspectives (see Fig. 10.2). It aims to demonstrate how the organisation meets the financial expectations of shareholders (Financial Perspective), how the right work is being done in the right way (Internal Process Perspective), how customers are satisfied (Customer Perspective) and how the organisation is ready for the future (Learning and Growth Perspective). The four

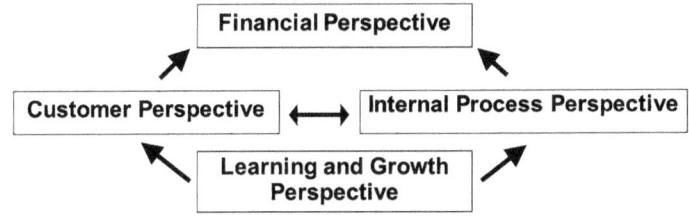

Fig. 10.2 A simplified balanced scorecard (BSC) (Modified from Kaplan and Norton 1992)

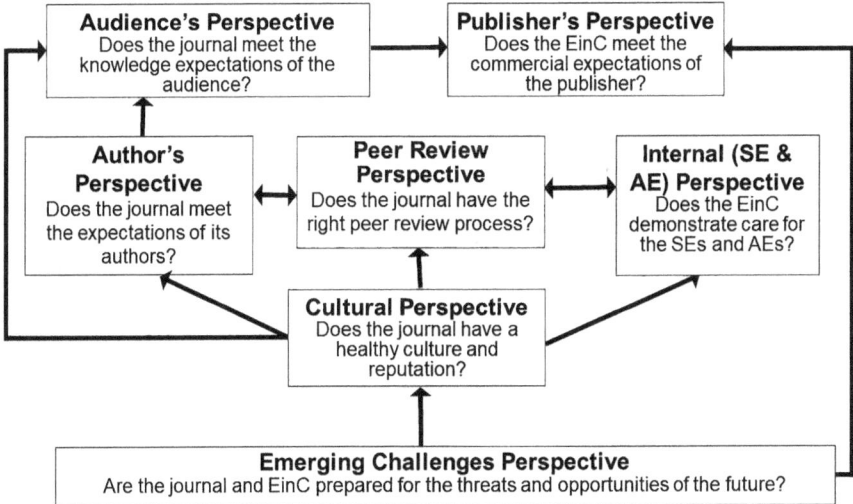

Fig. 10.3 A balanced scorecard for the EinC of an academic journal

perspectives are interlinked, with the arrows in Fig. 10.2 indicating influence-based relationships. For example, the Learning and Growth Perspective will include activities that help to enhance both the Internal Process Perspective and the Customer Perspective.

The BSC can be operationalised at different levels, i.e. a high-level strategic overview or a more detailed account. The BSC can even be applied at the level of the individual employee or manager. The BSC has also been adapted to different contexts; for instance, I worked on an adaptation of the BSC to the Information Systems context with my colleague Maris Martinsons in the late 1990s (Martinsons et al. 1999).

In thinking about the world of the EinC, and how the EinC can create a strategy, I adapted the original BSC in a radical way (see Fig. 10.3). While the

BSC traditionally has four perspectives, as in Fig. 10.2, I decided that to illustrate the nature of the EinC's world and the responsibilities therein, seven linked perspectives are needed. I consider this EinC BSC to constitute an important step in my journey to create a theory of editing. The seven perspectives correspond to the major activities that I cover in this book. Figure 10.3 thus captures, at a very high level, the essence of the EinC's remit, though of course not all the details, and as such can serve as a high-level guide to strategic directions. I must emphasise that the arrows do not imply direct (and positive) cause and effect relationships, but rather signify how the perspectives are associated with each other, or how undertaking the activities in one perspective may influence another perspective. The questions inside each box reflect the concerns that the EinC should have for each perspective and therefore should prompt further actions to ensure that the questions can be answered affirmatively.

The seven perspectives in Fig. 10.3 reflect that seven entities are central to the EinC's strategic planning efforts. Each of the seven includes a single question that is directed at either the EinC or the journal. Although the EinC is responsible for answering all these questions, the stakeholders may see the journal as the responsible party more than the EinC. Thus, for example, where the audience is concerned, the audience will ask if the journal (not the EinC) meets its expectations. On the other hand, where the publisher is concerned, it is indeed the EinC who is seen as the responsible party, given the contractual relationship between the editor and the publisher.

There are two perspectives at the top of the diagram, the Audience and the Publisher. This reflects how both the audience and the publisher are significant stakeholders for the EinC and the journal. The EinC needs to satisfy (meet the commercial expectations of) the publisher, and at the same time needs to satisfy (meet the knowledge expectations of) the audience. Meeting the audience's expectations will help to satisfy the publisher's expectations, because a satisfied audience is more likely to be downloading and citing articles (and thus generating income and a higher IF) that will contribute to the publisher's satisfaction.

In the centre of Fig. 10.3 there are three perspectives: the author, the peer review process and the internal (SE and AE). The EinC needs to manage these three entities carefully. Authors need to receive high-quality feedback on their submitted manuscripts in a timely fashion, which implies a relationship with the peer review process. The peer review process itself has to be carefully designed and managed so as to ensure that it operates smoothly and benefits the authors as it is used by the SEs and AEs. The SEs and AEs themselves must also be cared for by the EinC, in terms of ensuring that they are not overloaded and that the manuscripts assigned to them are within their areas of competence.

A key responsibility of the EinC relates to the creation of a culture, and the associated reputation, of the journal. The culture affects all aspects of how the journal is seen by its many different stakeholders, internal and external. The culture is visible in policy documents and editorials, and also informs the peer review process. For instance, the culture may specify that the peer review process should be constructive, polite, friendly, robust, etc. These values pertain to the culture, and then are reflected in the peer review process. The culture is also present in the communications that take place between the EinC and various stakeholders (authors, SEs and AEs, the audience), where special attention needs to be paid to the style and tone of communication, which may vary depending on the context and the person. Finally, at the bottom of Fig. 10.3, is the emerging challenges perspective. This accounts for the threats and opportunities that may affect the journal. *Current* examples include plagiarism, generative AI, alternative presentation modes, and the open access movement. EinCs need to scan the horizon for new threats and opportunities, as well as manage those that have already appeared. By engaging with these threats and opportunities, the EinC can ensure firstly that the culture of the journal will be kept up to date, and secondly that the publisher has the confidence that the EinC is prepared for the future situations that the journal may encounter, and thus will not be surprised by unforeseen circumstances. Arguably, the EinC also needs to develop emotional resilience to cope with these various pressures. The role of EinC is very much a labour of love.

Apart from this high level BSC, a lower level set of attributes can also be identified that help to push the BSC from the strategic to the operational. Figure 10.4 below outlines a matrix to illustrate how this may look in practice. Populating this matrix is a critical activity for each EinC and while I offer my own extended version of what this could look like in Appendix D, I must emphasise that even though there may be some commonalities across journals and hence BSCs, each EinC should approach this task independently. I need to observe that it is customary to populate the measures column of a BSC with items that are amenable to quantitative measurement, and for the targets to be numerical. However, in Appendix D I bend this rule to some extent as it is not always practical to have quantitative measures or targets. Nevertheless, I do not want my BSC to become a de facto standard that EinCs should follow. Each journal occupies its own intellectual niche and thus a BSC needs to be customised to the specific needs of that journal and its EinC(s).

The design of the template is premised not only on the seven perspectives, but also four dimensions: objectives, initiatives, measures and targets. In the

Perspective	Objectives	Initiatives	Measures	Targets
Audience				
Publisher				
Author				
Peer Review				
Internal				
Culture & Reputation				
Emerging Challenges				

Fig. 10.4 A scorecard template for the EinC of an academic journal

case of the EinC, the *objectives* are the goals that the EinC wants to achieve for each of the seven perspectives. The *initiatives* consist of the actions that the EinC proposes to take in order to achieve the objectives. The *measures* are the items that indicate how achievement of the objectives will be assessed. The *targets* involve how much of the measure and a date when the objective should be achieved. Populating this template, probably with several objectives, initiatives, measures and targets for each perspective, will push the EinC to think about the operational details of the strategy. Nevertheless, there are some essential rules that govern the relationships in the template. Firstly, it is critical is that the Objectives be concrete and realistic. They must be linked to the Initiatives by a cause-effect relationship, i.e. undertaking the actions implicit in the Initiative will have a direct consequence in terms of the Objective. The achievement of the Objective needs to be measured with something, ideally a quantitative measure that is easily and cheaply collected. Finally, the Target refers to how much of the Measure (describing the Objective) needs to be achieved and when. The Target could be an absolute number (of the measure) or it could be a percentage change. A date should be specified for each Target. It is more useful that the BSC be future oriented, so that it has planning and assessment value into the future. For instance, if I determine the objectives and identify the initiatives in mid-2024, then the target dates by when these objectives need to be met could be set at 2025, 2027 and 2030 for the short, medium and longer terms.

10.4 Discussion

The world of the EinC is multifaceted. It includes multiple activities that are important to multiple stakeholders. Some activities are regular or quotidian, others are irregular or occasional. As such, this world defies a parsimonious reduction to simple elements. Even the BSC that I develop above is moderately complex, while the WSS gives hints as to the complexity of operational processes. Although the fundamental task of the EinC is to manage the review of manuscripts, leading to acceptance of articles for publication, this task is underpinned by a huge range of subsidiary but critical tasks. Like Bob, who I briefly introduced at the start of this chapter, the EinC needs to be an expert in all aspects of the world, a master of all trades, a fount of knowledge about all processes with the memory of an elephant. As with the parable of the blind men and the elephant, an outside observer who interacted briefly with an EinC could only glimpse part of the totality of what it is that EinCs do, and thus a small segment of the theory of the EinC. Between them, the BSC and WSS that I develop above provide the best pictorial representation of the theory of the EinC that I can conjure up. The WSS lists the key tasks, technologies, information, products and customers. The BSC illustrates the nature of the relationships. In Appendix D I provide more details of the BSC, but these strictly lie beyond the formal statement of the theory itself as they are (mere) operational details.

EinCs need to be life-long learners. The material that I present in this book is drawn from my own experiences, and is also informed by the experiences of other editors who have read and commented on different versions of the text. I am immensely grateful to them for their time, energy and thoughts. Entire new chapters were written after receiving that feedback. The text of the book is much longer and more detailed as a result. Although the theory that I present in this chapter is complete today, it can never be final. I suggest it as the basis for how editors of all kinds could frame their work, yet each editor will have experiences that to a greater or lesser extent vary from those that I describe here, and thus the way that they might create a WSS or BSC could also vary. A definitive theory of an EinC is a chimera: it doesn't exist. A theory can only exist at the level of its creator. Naturally, a theory can be tested, checked, improved, modified or debunked at any stage. I hope that the theory I present here, notwithstanding its subjective origins, will inspire other editors to reconsider their craft and improve it, for we will all benefit from that as it will lead to enhanced manuscript review processes, culture, reputation and thus contribution to progress.

Appendices

Appendix A: Templates for Decision Letters and Other Communications

Desk Reject Template Options

Dear Authors,

   Thank you for submitting your work to XXX. At this journal, it is customary that we screen all submissions. Based on this screening we decide whether or not the submission should be sent for review.

   Following my reading of the submission, I think that it needs to be significantly developed if it is to survive the review process at this journal.

   The main issue with the manuscript is …

> …that the theoretical contribution is very limited. To give you a sense of our expectations, please refer to a recent editorial at this journal (link) where we highlight the need for Research Manuscripts to have a strong theoretical contribution for them to be publishable at this journal.

> …that the methods have not been applied appropriately. For instance, you indicate that you are employing an interpretive case study, but your methods, references and arguments are appropriate for a positive case study. OR … you indicate that you are employing Action Research, but you fail to appreciate that there are many different forms of Action Research and it is not clear which form you are using.

… that a considerable amount of the contemporary literature on XXX has been omitted, with the result that your research models are poorly informed and justified.

… that your data analysis techniques are out of date/inappropriate/incomplete, with the result that we cannot have confidence in your findings.

In sum, I regret to say that I do not see any specific details in this submission that will attract the interest of the IS research community. The issues that I identify above can be addressed, but this will require revisiting your research design and the collection of new data. The outcome of those changes will be a new manuscript. I do encourage the authors to read articles published in this journal so as to develop a sense of our benchmarks.

We are sensitive to your need for a timely decision. Although you will certainly be disappointed with the outcome of this review, given the weaknesses in the manuscript it is likely that reviewers would have recommended rejection of the manuscript. Thank you for considering 'XXX' as a venue for your research. We look forward to the opportunity of reviewing your best work in future.

Reject After Reviews

Dear Authors.

Thank you for submitting your work to XXX. Following our receipt of the manuscript, I assigned it to a Senior Editor who has in turn recruited an Associate Editor and three reviewers. I think that you will agree with me that the quality of their reviews is outstanding.

The review team unanimously agrees that your research topic and problem are in scope for this journal, and indeed are also worthy of investigation. Further we agree that your application of a survey/case study/ethnographic/action research approach is viable. However, we unfortunately regret to advise that your research design has fatal flaws, as exemplified by Reviewer 2 and the AE. As a result, I regret to inform you that we are not asking you to revise your manuscript but are rejecting it from the review process.

Although you will certainly be disappointed with the outcome of this review, I hope that you will find the review team's feedback helpful as you consider how to continue your work in this domain.

Special Issue Reject Template

Dear Dr. X.

Many thanks for proposing a special issue on XX for the XX.

I have reviewed your special issue proposal carefully and I regret to inform you that I have decided not to accept it. I suggest that the topic is not appropriate for this journal and it would be more suitable if you considered a journal in the following domain: XXX.

I also note that the three proposed guest editors of the special issue have never published their research either in this journal or other journals in this discipline. Instead, your Google Scholar pages indicate that all three of you publish primarily in XX, YY and ZZ disciplines.

Finally, I was puzzled to see that you suggested an initial submission date that is only 2 months from now, with a final decision date only 9 months from now. Your proposed timetable only allows for a single round of revision. I think it is unlikely that an appropriate level of quality will be achieved in manuscripts that are subject to such a tight schedule. At this journal, accepted manuscripts are, on average, revised four times prior to acceptance, a process that on average requires 22 months.

I suggest that in future you look carefully at the guidelines for special issues which you can find at this link: XX.

Special Issue Accept Template

Dear Dr. X.

Many thanks for proposing a special issue on XX to XX.

I have read your proposal carefully and find that it is both in scope for this journal and likely to attract high quality submissions. Your proposed team of guest Senior and Associate Editors are highly qualified individuals, many of whom have published in this journal previously, as well as in other journals in this domain. I am particularly impressed that you have been able to secure the services of Dr. G as a guest Senior Editor and Dr. P as a guest Associate Editor. Your list of authors who may be interested to submit is good, though I note a strong European bias and I suggest that you may promote the special issue globally.

At this stage, I am going to send your proposal to the Senior and Associate Editors of the journal for their additional feedback. It is our policy at this journal to invite our regular SEs and AEs to serve on special issues. Their participation helps to ensure that we maintain our standards. I will return their details comments to you within the next 2 weeks, at which time you can convert this proposal into a formal call for manuscripts.

Revise and Resubmit (Major or Minor) Template

Dear Authors.

Thank you for submitting your work to XXX. Following our receipt of the manuscript, I assigned it to a Senior Editor who has in turn recruited an Associate Editor and three reviewers. I think that you will agree with me that the quality of their reviews is outstanding.

Having considered the reviews and the Senior and Associate Editor reports, I am delighted to offer you the opportunity to revise the manuscript. I expect that you will engage with the reviews, reflecting carefully on how you can revise your manuscript. It is not essential that you do everything that is asked for, but it is critical that you prepare a detailed revision document in which you respond to every comment that the review team makes. If you disagree with any of the recommended changes or observations, please document and justify your position carefully. Please also feel free to reach out to me in case any of the comments are not clear, or you are not sure how to proceed.

I note that Reviewer 3 has some concerns about the methodology. However, I do not want to see an extended tutorial on the methodology included in the revision as this will unnecessarily lengthen the manuscript and diffuse the focus. You may refer to this observation from myself when you write up the revision notes.

Given the magnitude of the changes, I am setting a resubmission deadline 9 months from today, but if you need more time please let me know.

Accept Letter Template

Dear Authors.

Many thanks for further revising your manuscript. I am now delighted to report that the entire review team endorses the decision to accept your manuscript without further modification.

Many thanks for further revising your manuscript. In this round I have consulted the Senior Editor and together we have reached the decision to accept your manuscript without further modification.

Many thanks for further revising your manuscript. The review team is, as in the previous round, still split with one reviewer arguing that the submission should be rejected, but the other members of the team arguing for acceptance. After careful consideration with the Senior Editor, I have decided that we will not be seeking further changes and have decided to accept your manuscript at this juncture.

Please accept my congratulations. We look forward to seeing the final version online very soon.

Response Options for an Individual Who Self-Nominates for an SE or AE Position

Dear Dr. X.

Many thanks for your email in which you expressed an interest in serving as an AE/SE at this journal.

We normally appoint new AEs from among those people who have already reviewed for the journal and also published articles in the journal, as well as similar journals. The reason for this normal process is that we believe that people who are already familiar with our standards will be more suitable to work as AEs.

We normally appoint SEs from among the best of our AEs, i.e. AEs who have served the journal with distinction for several years.

I have checked our records and find that you have no account on our MMS, and therefore have never reviewed for this journal nor submitted your work to this journal. I suggest that for this reason, you are not qualified for an AE or SE position. I further suggest that you consider creating an account on the MMS where you indicate the keywords that most accurately reflect your skills so that we can invite you to be a reviewer in the future. Please also consider submitting your best work to us.

I have checked our records and find that while you do have an account on our MMS, you have never submitted a manuscript to us. We have invited you to undertake two reviews for us over the last few years. You always accepted our invitations to review, but on one occasion you did not deliver the review despite multiple reminders and on another occasion your review was finally delivered 3 months after the deadline. Please understand that we owe a duty of care to our authors, and part of this care relates to completing reviews on time. For this reason, I do not believe that it is appropriate for us to offer you an AE position.

Appendix B: Index and Brief Summary of Selected Editorials (in Alphabetical Order) Note: All Editorials Can Be Downloaded at no Charge from the Wiley Online Library[1]

Topic	Brief description
An eye for detail	Details are important because they help the reader to make sense of the situation that is being described. however, not all authors seem willing to provide details even when asked repeatedly. I understand that there may be privacy issues and that too much detail could compromise privacy but a complete absence of detail makes interpretation of research very difficult. I strongly encourage authors to provide as much detail as they reasonably can, and indeed for reviewers to request this.
Appreciating alien thinking	Editors are no more omniscient than anyone else, i.e. we have our limitations and gaps in knowledge. We can't be experts in all topics, methods, epistemologies, etc. but at the same time, we can't be constrained by our failure to understand the work of others. Thus, I argue that we need to learn to appreciate and accept the legitimacy of very different ways of thinking. In some respects, the EinC of a journal needs to be a diplomat: You need to interact with people whom you may not only not understand, but also cordially disagree with. Yet you cannot reach a decision on a manuscript solely based on your personal preferences: There needs to be a more objective set of criteria that you apply to the evaluation process.
Conflicts of interest	Conflicts of interest are almost endemic in research communities, where many people know each other, work together, etc. The more extensive your network, whether of colleagues or co-authors, so the greater the number of conflicts of interest that will occur. As EinC I try very hard to mitigate these conflicts, but it inevitably happens that I send reject decisions to people I know. Some take these decisions well, but others … may be offended or worse. There can also be (I hope unintentional) conflicts in review teams where the authors are related to the reviewers of their manuscripts, usually because they are recent co-authors or in a supervisor/supervisee relationship. We try to avoid such conflicts, but lapses do happen.

---

[1] https://onlinelibrary.wiley.com/page/journal/13652575/homepage/editorials.htm

Constructive reviewing	We expect reviewers to offer critical but constructive advice in a polite way. It is more helpful to provide actionable advice that the authors can do something with, not polemical arguments that may express the reviewer's opinion yet cannot be acted on. Instead of assuming the responsibility to reject, I invite reviewers to try and identify what needs to be changed for a manuscript to be accepted.
Context	All research is undertaken in some context, but it is not always clearly specified. as a result, readers may struggle to interpret the findings. I argue for more transparency where contextual details are concerned. this has implications for the extent to which research findings can reasonably be generalised beyond their immediate context.
Cultural bias in reviews	I find that reviewers are sometimes biased which is unfair to authors and impedes the publication of high-quality research. It is important to invite reviewers who are familiar with the methods employed by the authors. It is also important that reviewers be open minded about research, such that they can see the merits in research designs or that are conducted in social contexts with which they are not familiar.
Diversity	Diversity is a critical attribute of a journal, in my view. IS a broad field, with many different topics, approaches, theories, methods. It is important that our editorial teams are diverse, and thus competent to handle a diversity of research that may be submitted. but I am also looking for diversity beyond research: I would like the SEs and AEs themselves to be diverse in terms of their own cultural backgrounds, and other demographic indicators. By being geographically diverse, we send the message to authors that we welcome research from a diversity of people as well.

Do scholarly journals have cultural values?	I argue that they do, and that these values shape what the journal is known for. For my part, I see these values as encompassing such issues as the care that we demonstrate towards different stakeholders, e.g. authors, reviewers, SEs and AEs, readers. Care here refers to the quality of our interactions, i.e. we should provide authors with high quality, constructive and actionable feedback that helps them improve their work. Care also refers to how we help AEs and SEs develop their skills in their roles, and how we don't overload them with tasks. I see the people associated with the journals I edit as members of a family: people here includes the SEs and AEs, but also the reviewers and the authors. As a family, we work together on publishing a manuscript. Yes, of course, the authors take the leading and most prominent role, but the review team members play an important role as well.
Established theory rejection	Theoretical novelty is a tricky topic in research. Many editors and journals have a strong expectation of novelty, and consequently have a less rosy view of replication. At the same time, theories that are developed but never again used have very limited value. It is important to validate theory through multiple applications, yet as the numbers rise so the incremental value of each new study declines. Some theories have reached the point where the number of replications is in the thousands, and here it seems futile to continue: The theory is well established, essentially unchallenged, and so further theoretical nuance is very hard to achieve except in a study that debunks the theory completely.

For whom do we write?	Authors may write for themselves, for an audience, or for the limited set of people on a review team. Some authors are highly selective about their audience, others are more open. Some have a particular audience in mind when they write and target that audience through a particular journal. Others are less targeted. Some authors commented that while in the initial version of a manuscript, they write as they would like to write, the pressure of reviewer comment that emerges during the review-revision process means that in the end they are only writing for the reviewers and hope to satisfy them. In my view, that's sad, and it reflects a problem with the review process, namely that the authors have to satisfy all reviewers before a manuscript can be accepted. Personally, I don't agree with such an arrangement and instead argue that SEs and AEs have the prerogative to decide when a manuscript should be accepted. Moreover, they can reach this decision even when some reviewers are holding out for more revisions.
From ignorance to familiarity	A researcher in any field is likely to be an expert in the topic, method, theory. But how do they achieve such expertise? It seems unlikely that they were born like this! When you read a research manuscript, authors very seldom explain in any detail how they became familiar with the context, and so they appear to be instant experts. I find this confusing and I can imagine that PhD students and junior scholars in particular may find this lack of explanation quite frustrating: They too need to learn how to become experts, but the experts are not telling them how they achieved their expert familiarity in the field. In this editorial, I argue that authors would do us all a service by being more transparent about how they acquired knowledge in a given research domain.
Iconoclasm	Iconoclasm strictly refers to the breaking of icons. In a research sense, the icons are the established theories, practices, principles and perhaps people. Iconoclastic research thus refers to challenges to the status quo, to established practices, all of which are implicitly associated with people. The challenges should also incorporate new ways of thinking or working, new ideas or theories, new methods, analytical techniques or tools that facilitate the research. Iconoclasm is not for everyone, but it is an important part of the research process.

Impact and implications for practice	It is important that the research we do has impact for the relevant stakeholders. Much of the time, it appears that these stakeholders are limited to other researchers, yet increasingly we find that authors are considering the impact that their research has in the non-research world of practice. Unfortunately, the beneficiaries of this impact are often lumped together as 'managers', with little consideration for other stakeholders, notably employees, citizens and the environment. Creating awareness about the different kinds of impact that can exist is one step on the road to changing a discipline from one that is only concerned with itself and its own people to one that sees its responsibilities in terms of a broader audience.
Impact factors	Although they are maligned for ignoring the impact of individual research articles, impact factors are still used as a popular proxy for quality at the level of the journal. in this editorial, we explore the world of impact factors in considerable detail, and examine some of the trends that we can see. We note for instance how a single research article can cause a significant spike (i.e. a temporary rise) in the impact factor of a journal to the extent that one article may contribute to more than 50% of a journal's impact factor in a given year. We also observe how editors can to some extent 'game' the way impact factors are calculated.

Importance of context	When I read an empirical research article, I would like to know where the research was done and the data was collected, and who or what is described in that data. This means that I want to know the context of the research. Unfortunately, many authors are coy with regard to context, either ignoring it altogether or providing so few details that it cannot reliably be guessed at. When challenged for their reticence, they provide such excuses as 'the research findings are universally applicable, so it doesn't matter where the data was collected' or 'no one is interested in the country where we collected data, so we decided not to mention this'[!!]. I argue in this editorial that context is actually very important, that research findings are by no means automatically universal, and so that it does matter very much where the data was collected. Knowing where the research was undertaken and what the data describes helps me to make sense of the research findings. If I am a practitioner, that sense making is critical to my recontextualisation of the findings, i.e. can I use them in my own work, or are they so far removed from what I do that I should ignore them?
Indigenous theory	Aligned with context is the issue of indigeneity. In this editorial, I promoted the idea that we should value new theory that is situated in a particular cultural context. this implies that the theory may not be universal; instead, it may be very local. However, it is not less valuable for this reason. In fact, it may be more useful because people in that cultural context will know that it describes a situation that is culturally compatible, and that they can rely on it. Meanwhile, researchers have the opportunity to learn about the cultural concepts of another culture and they can either borrow or adapt these new concepts and see if they also apply in their own context.
Journal characteristics	Although journals have roughly the same mission, i.e. to publish research and thus to advance knowledge, each journal has its own characteristics. Indeed, authors often select a journal because of those characteristics, which may contribute to the journal's fame or notoriety. At the journals I edit, these characteristics relate most prominently to the nature of the review process, which we want to be constructive, polite, friendly and helpful.

Novelty	Why are novel contributions particularly welcome? A key objective of research is to advance knowledge and one way to achieve that is through novel research designs, novel theoretical contributions, and novel approaches to problem solving.
On serendipity: The happy discovery of unsought knowledge	Most research is carefully planned, meticulously executed. Occasionally, the authors don't find what they expect to find, or find something quite unexpected. The latter kind of discovery is intriguing and can lead to significant contributions to knowledge, if the author is receptive to this. As EinC I encourage authors not only to report on what they expected to find, but also on the unexpected, the serendipitous.
Peer review process	The peer review process is acknowledged to be flawed, yet it is also critical because of the central role that it plays in the evaluation of research. In this editorial I highlight some of the problems and emphasise the duty of care that editors owe to authors.
Pickled eggs: Generative AI as research assistant or co-author?	Generative AI has been a major discussion point since 2023 and many scholars and pundits have voiced their predictions, both rosy and dire, for the impacts that may yet unfold. We explore a few of the issues, as they pertain to research, as a contribution to the debate. The maturity of the technology continues to develop, yet the number of errors means that authors must be particularly careful to ensure that they own all their content, as only they can be responsible for it.
Predatory journals	This is a tricky topic, because there is no agreement on exactly what constitutes a predatory journal and labelling a journal or its publisher as predatory may invite legal consequences. Nevertheless, the debate about predatory publishing practices is important since there are recognised threats to the research establishment and junior authors in particular may inadvertently find themselves caught up in snares that can damage their careers.

Quirks, neologisms, provocations and the mundane: Titles and interpretations	Here I deal with the titles that authors create for their manuscripts. I suggest that titles are intrinsically important. While some authors attempt to cram all the salient aspects of their manuscript into the title, others create titles that may seem bizarre or quirky, attracting readers accordingly. Some titles involve catachresis, i.e. juxtaposing ideas in new ways, and others include neologisms, i.e. words that they have invented for the purpose of describing their research. While some titles are several lines long, others may be limited to a few words. My objective is to encourage more creativity in title formation.
Research problematisation	We argue that instead of looking for 'gaps' in the literature, authors should problematise their research designs and questions, seeking to advance knowledge by identifying a real problem situation that is relevant to real stakeholders, and then investigating that situation in a novel way that leads to the creation of knowledge that goes beyond what is already known about the phenomenon.
Researchers and the stakeholders' perspective	Who are the beneficiaries of research? Whose perspectives do the authors choose to prioritise or focus on? In the vast majority of cases, I find that authors limit themselves to the economic interests of the organisation. Social or hedonic interests are considered to a much lesser extent. Meanwhile, other stakeholders, such as employees and citizens, as well as NGOs, see very little research attention. The environment, and environmental issues, are almost never considered. There are moves to encourage research on sustainability, but much of this research amounts to little more than helping improve the public image of corporations by burnishing their green credentials. The net benefits for the environment, if any, are not reported. I argue in this editorial that there is a need to diversify away from both the economic and the corporate perspective. Although they are legitimate, so too are other perspectives.

126   **Appendices**

Responsible research	Are we making the world a better place as a result of our research? It depends on how we define 'the world'. If we limit to the world of the corporate stakeholder, then very often the answer is 'yes'. But if we are referring to the natural world, the answer is rarely 'yes'. In this editorial that prefaces a special issue on the topic, I argue for a more carefully considered debate about our responsibilities as researchers and suggest that we aim to consider how we can make the world a better place.
Scholarly conversation through a review response document	I encourage authors to engage in a conversation with the review team through the response document that they create as they address the reviewer comments. Although many authors may imagine that they simply have to do everything that the review team asks for, I suggest that a more nuanced approach is possible, and desirable. Although the conversation cannot be a natural one, mediated as it is by the formalities of the review process and expressed in the form of a written document, I hope that both reviewers and authors can express themselves in a friendly and conversational manner. This then leads to situations where if, for example, the authors disagree with the reviewer comments, they can say so, if they argue for their own perspective in a careful and reasonable manner. This style of communication was brought home to me by a senior editor (where I was the author of the manuscript) who told me 'I actually don't expect that you will do everything that we ask for, but I would like you to react to our comments and express your opinion. Don't just ignore the bits that you don't like'.
SE and AE roles	The nature of the SE and AE roles in a journal is seldom spelled out in much detail. Journal websites tend to restrict themselves to guidelines for authors and reviewers, but rarely for the editors. We suggest that these two roles are quite distinct (though they may be combined at journals that have only one of these two positions), with a clear division of responsibilities. Nevertheless, I encourage SEs and AEs to engage in a conversation throughout the review process. It is not just a matter of the SE assigning the manuscript to the AE and waiting for something to happen. The SE has a mentoring role, but both of them need to form an opinion about the manuscript that they are handling.

Shifting baselines in IS research threaten our future relevance	In any research discipline, it is likely that over time the standards of what is normal or acceptable shift. The shifts may be more or less dramatic in scope. Some may reflect changes in accepted practices regarding methodology, or theory, or the analysis of data. The standards that were familiar 30 or more years ago may have fallen by the wayside and been replaced by more contemporary perspectives. These shifts, however, are not solely the purview of the authors who need to keep up to date. They are also in scope for journal editors, but in this they create a problem. Should the editor move with the times, adjusting the standards for what is acceptable practice? Or are there situations where the editor should hold on to past practice? In my own discipline, it used to be the case (and many authors still hold on to this practice) that in a research article there is the expectation for a theoretical contribution to be made. However, some researchers appear to be abandoning theory altogether, and are submitting manuscripts that are essentially atheoretical. These latter manuscripts often involve the analysis of big data sets, for instance the hunting for correlations. It is likely that generative AI programmes may well help researchers to do this kind of analysis. Some journals are accepting this kind of research, but others insist that a theoretical contribution is essential and the absence of theory means that the manuscript is not publishable. Quite how this situation will play out is hard to foretell at the moment, but there is naturally the risk that if the majority of researchers tend to the newer trend, with ever fewer (in this case) seeking to make theoretical contributions, then either the journal changes or it ceases to exist.
Storytelling	Storytelling is a powerful way of telling readers about the research. Stories can function as tools for learning and action. A well-told story can be a delight to read, and the research is likely to be remembered. Stories need to include details, and this means that they should be complete. Don't truncate the methods or the false starts: we want to learn what worked well and what was less successful.

The art of referencing	References are a key part of the academic writing process. We give credit to those who came before us, the giants on whose shoulders we stand. But we do not encourage name dropping practices, where authors might cite a dozen or so manuscripts in support of a single point. Referencing thus needs to be undertaken carefully. We also shun coercive referencing practices, where editors insist that authors should cite specific articles (often authored by themselves). Such coercive referencing is utterly unethical, though we recognise its existence. I was the victim of a coercive referencing requirement early in my career when I was informed that my manuscript would be accepted if I cited six specific articles. None of the six were particularly relevant to the manuscript I was writing, yet I tried to do so more or less coherently, not realising how I was being inveigled into an unethical practice. Each of the six articles was authored by the editor of the journal or his students.
The limitations of limitations	The limitations section at the end of a research manuscript is a useful place to reflect on what went wrong in the research, and what could have been done better. This often links to future research, i.e. what still needs to be done. However, some authors have developed the tendency to take a template approach to limitations. They bewail the limitations of their intentional research design ('we apologise for collecting cross-sectional survey data: future researchers should conduct longitudinal studies') in one country ('a multi-country study would be better') or even for using a particular method. These kinds of limitations are disingenuous because they are no more than what the researchers planned to do in the first place. Also, I find that later studies repeat the same limitations, i.e. no one actually learns from them, or does things any better, so these are essentially fake limitations. I encourage authors to be more honest in identifying their limitations.

Titles matter	Titles vary from the short and pithy to the long and detailed. Some are almost as long as the abstract, others are but a few words, yet are equally able to convey the substance of the research. The selection of a title is a personal matter, one that reviewers seldom comment on. But getting the title 'right' is important because this is very often what most readers will remember, and so a carefully crafted title may cause the article itself to be remembered far longer. In this editorial I provide several examples of memorable titles and encourage both authors to consider their titles carefully, and reviewers to engage with the title as much as the rest of the manuscript.
Why are you submitting to this journal?	Sometimes I wonder why an author submits a manuscript to a particular journal. The manuscript may be completely out of scope, but that does not seem to deter authors. The authors may completely ignore the author guidelines and as a result fail to include much information that would strengthen the manuscript. Some manuscripts have obviously been rejected from one or more journals previously, and they will be rejected from this one too and for the same reasons. Do authors reason why this journal and this audience is the right one for the manuscript they are writing? One of my colleagues told me that she submits a manuscript to a journal because she wants to influence the audience of that the journal, the people who habitually read that journal. I think that this is an excellent selection criterion. It demonstrates the awareness that the audience can vary, which indeed it does.

Why theory matters

In some ways, this editorial is linked to others that I describe above, notably shifting baselines. Personally, I believe that theory is important and that in a research article it is reasonable for us to expect that authors will make a contribution to theory. We reject many manuscripts that fail to make such a contribution. My definition of a theory is 'a way of making sense of the world'. This is a broad definition that can include many types of theory. Some may be cause and effect theories, i.e. if you do this then there will be some consequences. Others are explanatory, as they seek to explain how things happen. Some theories are purely descriptive, yet they all invoke the essential contribution of making sense of a situation. Theories can help us to plan, to organise, to explain. We can test them, improve them, rebut them, debunk them and create new theories. Few theories last forever, but for the extent of its lifetime a theory helps people to understand a situation, and perhaps to make sense of their lives. In an applied discipline like information systems, a theory provides an anchor that helps us to tie down our ideas.

Appendix C: A List of Files that I Maintain

Accepted articles A more detailed report can be obtained from the publisher indicating in addition such details as number of downloads and citations on an annual basis, as well as gender and location of the first author.	A complete detailed list of all articles that have been accepted for publication since the start of my tenure as EinC. the file includes: Digital object identifier (DOI). Number of volume and issue where the published manuscript appears. Original manuscript submission number. First author name. Article title. Date of appearance online (early view). Date of assignment to an issue. Lapsed time (in months) from appearance online to assignment to an issue.
Archive	A complete archive of all articles published (ever) in the journals that I edit in PDF.
Contacts	Contact details for all SEs, AEs and EAB members. For demographic purposes (i.e. so as to be aware of diversity issues) I also keep details of their gender (self-described), ethnicity (self-described), the country(ies) where they studied for their PhD, where they were born and where they are currently working. Individuals can choose to withhold this information.
Guidelines	Detailed guidelines for authors, reviewers, SEs and AEs, and the proposers of special issues. Author guidelines include detailed descriptions of manuscript types. Reviewer guidelines include links to publisher resources and editorials related to the role of editors. SE and AE guidelines are designed for newly appointed people so as to provide a checklist of their responsibilities. Special issue guidelines include a checklist of items required in a special issue proposal.

Impact factors	A detailed list of the IFs of 20 journals in the discipline where the journals that I edit are located. I maintain this comparative data for all these journals (extracted from publicly available Clarivate resources) from 2010 onwards so as to be able to chart the evolution of IFs over time. I also keep data on which articles make significant contributions to IFs, which articles contribute the most citations to IFs, and other details. More detailed descriptions and analysis can be found in Davison and Lowry (2023).
Keywords	A detailed list of keywords for all SEs and AEs. The purpose is to be able to identify the areas of expertise of each SE and AE. These keywords are provided by the SEs and AEs directly. They include topics, methods, epistemology, etc. I refer to the keywords when assigning manuscripts to SEs. I make this information available to SEs so as to help them with AE assignments.
Manuscripts in process	A complete list of all manuscripts that are currently under review in the journal.
Special issue lists	The calls for manuscripts for all current and former special issues. It is useful to refer to these when new special issues are proposed.
Special issue teams	A list of all the SEs and AEs who are associated with each special issue. A separate file indicates which of the regular SEs and AEs are working on special issues. This helps me to ensure that a small number of people are not overly influential in contributing to the review teams associated with special issues.
Special issue status	A list of all manuscripts submitted to each special issue with an indication of each manuscript's current status, i.e. under review, major or minor revisions in progress, accepted for publication, or rejected.
Workloads	A file with details updated on a monthly basis about how many manuscripts each SE and AE is handling, as well as annual totals, back dated to the start of my tenure as EinC. I do not keep data on special issue editorial teams unless those people are also regular SEs and AEs.

Appendix D: A Balanced Scorecard for an Editor in Chief

Perspective	Objectives	Initiatives	Measures	Targets
Audience	1. To publish articles that … (a) Make novel contributions to the academic literature (b) Offer practical recommendations for practitioners (c) Challenge the status quo	1. Establish criteria for acceptance that are predicated on and celebrate novel and practical contributions 2. Communicate these criteria to the review team members (SEs, AEs, reviewers) 3. Communicate expectations to authors and encourage them to submit work that is novel and/or makes practical contributions to knowledge	1. A novelty index 2. A practicality index	At least 80% of the articles accepted for publication should be demonstrably novel with respect to some aspect of method, theory or practice, by 2025
Publisher	1. To meet or exceed the publisher's expectations with regard to… (a) the number of articles published each year (b) the impact of the articles published	1. Work with authors to help them to achieve the required standards for publication 2. Encourage editors to be constructive when handling manuscripts 3. Headhunt authors to contribute manuscripts on high impact topics	1. Publisher quota of articles expected to be accepted 2. Publisher expectation with regard to impact metrics	1. Meet or exceed the quota 2. Meet or exceed the impact metrics

Stakeholder	Objectives	Measures	Targets
Author	1. To create in the minds of the authors an understanding of what kind of research the journal welcomes	1. Communicate to the authors what kind of research is desired, through guidelines and editorials, submission instructions, special issue descriptions and feedback on submitted manuscripts	1. The extent to which submitted research conforms to the journal's expectations	1. 100% conformance
Peer review	1. To establish a peer review process that is employed by peer review teams to evaluate submitted manuscripts fairly and comprehensively, without bias or preference, leading to the provision of constructive feedback for authors	1. Benchmark the peer review practices against exemplar journals in the same field 2. Ensure compliance with the process by members of review teams 3. Enhance the peer review process as feedback is received or as weaknesses are identified 4. Monitor the peer review process for irregularities	1. Quality of reviews that are sent to authors 2. Consistency with the guidelines of those reviews 3. Conflicts of interest between authors and review team members	1. Authors are 100% satisfied with the quality of reviews, irrespective of the outcome 2. Review team members consistently uphold the standards of the peer review process 3. Conflicts of interest are kept to an absolute minimum or eliminated
Internal (SE and AE)	1. Help SEs and AEs to manage their workloads 2. Enable SEs and AEs to develop their expertise and careers	1. Collect data on how many manuscripts SEs and AEs are concurrently managing, and then assign manuscripts to them accordingly 2. Encourage SEs and AEs to take on more difficult manuscripts or those that lie outside their comfort zone	1. Monthly/annual totals of handled manuscripts 2. Count of how many manuscripts are assigned on topics outside the SEs and AEs comfort zones	1. SEs not to handle more than 3 manuscripts a month 2. AEs not to handle more than 1 manuscript a month 3. SEs and AEs not to handle more than 2 manuscripts a year outside their comfort zone

Culture and reputation	1. Develop and maintain a culture of inclusiveness and diversity across all the journal's stakeholders 2. Develop and maintain a reputation for quality across all the journal's stakeholders 3. Communicate the culture and reputation with all stakeholders 4. Communicate about newly published articles with all stakeholders	1. Proactively seek to identify and promulgate cultural factors that will enhance the quality of the journal and the published research 2. Encourage the SEs and AEs to contribute to the identification of these cultural factors 3. Adhere consistently to the journal's standards 4. Promote the journal to its stakeholders	1. Extent of SE and AE involvement in the journal's cultural development	1. All SEs are expected to play a role in building the journal's culture. AEs are welcome to do so as they mature in their roles
Emerging challenges and opportunities	1. Be prepared for the competitive landscape of the future 2. Familiarity with the emerging technology literature and the best practices of competitor journals 3. Maintain close contact with the journal's stakeholders 4. Develop the emotional resilience to cope with the pressures of being an EinC!	1. Scan the horizon for emerging issues that may affect the journal's future success 2. Engage with opportunities and threats as they arise in order to secure the best outcome for the journal 3. Develop professional networks with all journal-linked stakeholders	1. Depth and breadth of the EinC's network in all stakeholder groups relevant to the journal	1. No quantitative target, but no stakeholder group should be unrepresented in the EinC's network

References

Alter S (2013) Work system theory: overview of core concepts, extensions, and challenges for the future. J AIS 14(2):72–121

Alvesson M, Sandberg J (2011) Generating research questions through problematization. Acad Manag Rev 36(2):247–271

Bacon F (1620) Novum Organum. https://en.wikipedia.org/wiki/Novum_Organum

Barley SR (2006) When I write my masterpiece: thoughts on what makes a manuscript interesting. Acad Manag J 49(1):16–20

Baruch Y, Konrad A, Aguinis H, Starbuck W (eds) (2008) Opening the black box of editorship. Macmillan, London

Berns G (2010) Iconoclast: a neuroscientist reveals how to think differently. Boston, MA: Harvard Business School Publishing

Chatterjee S, Davison RM (2021) The need for compelling problematization in research: the prevalence of the gap-spotting approach and its limitations. Inf Syst J 31(2):227–230

Clarke R, Davison RM (2020) Through whose eyes? The critical concept of researcher perspective. J AIS 21(2):483–501

Davison RM (2002) Cultural complications of ERP. Commun ACM 45(7):109–111

Davison RM (2014) Cultural bias in reviews and mitigation options. Inf Syst J 24(6):475–477

Davison RM (2017a) The limitations of limitations. Inf Syst J 27(6):695–697

Davison RM (2017b) Appreciating alien thinking. Inf Syst J 27(2):121–124

Davison RM (2019) For whom do we write? Inf Syst J 29(3):577–581

Davison RM (2020a) Which journal characteristics best invite submissions? Inf Syst J 30(2):1–5

Davison RM (2020b) Research contributions: the role of the iconoclast. Inf Syst J 30(2):215–219

Davison RM (2021a) Diversity and inclusion at the EJISDC. Electron J Inf Syst Dev Countr 87(3):1–5

Davison RM (2021b) Diversity and inclusion at the ISJ. Inf Syst J 31(3):347–355

Davison RM, Lowry PB (2023) Addressing the implications of recent developments in journal impact factors. Inf Syst J 33(3):419–436

Davison RM, Martinsons MG (2016) Context is king! Considering particularism in research design and reporting. J Inf Technol 31(3):241–249

Davison RM, Nielsen P (2020) Predatory journals: a sign of an unhealthy publish or perish game? Inf Syst J 30(4):635–638

Davison RM, Tarafdar M (2018) Shifting baselines in information systems research threaten our future relevance. Inf Syst J 28(4):587–591

Davison RM, Tarafdar M (2022) Do scholarly journals have cultural values? Inf Syst J 32(5):927–931

Davison RM, de Vreede GJ, Briggs RO (2005) On peer review standards for the information systems literature. Commun AIS 16(49):967–980

Davison RM, Ou CXJ, Martinsons MG (2013) Information technology to support informal knowledge sharing. Inf Syst J 23(1):89–109

Davison RM, Ou CXJ, Ng E (2020) Inadequate information systems and organizational citizenship behavior. Inf Manag 57(6):1–10

Davison RM, Wong LHM, Ou CXJ, Alter S (2021) The coordination of workarounds: insights from responses to misfits between local realities and a mandated enterprise system. Inf Manag 58(8):1–12

Davison RM, Majchrzak A, Hardin AM, Ravishankar MN (2023a) Special issue on responsible IS research for a better world. Inf Syst J 33(1):1–7

Davison RM, Laumer S, Wong LHM, Tarafdar M (2023b) Pickled eggs: generative AI as research assistant or co-author. Inf Syst J 33(5):989–994

Descola P (1996) The spears of twilight: life and death in the Amazonian jungle. The Free Press, New York

Díaz Andrade A (2023) Dancing between theory and data: Abductive reasoning. In: Davison RM (ed) Handbook of qualitative research methods for information systems. Edward Elgar, Cheltenham, pp 274–287

Díaz Andrade A, Tarafdar M, Davison RM, Hardin A, Techatassanasoontorn AA, Lowry PB, Chatterjee S, Schwabe G (2023) The importance of theory at the ISJ. Inf Syst J 33(4):693–702

Dubin R (1978) Theory development. Free Press, New York

Dwivedi YK, Kshetri N, Hughes L, Slade ES, Jeyaraj A, Kar AK, Baabdullah AM, Koohang A, Raghavan V, Ahuja M, Albanna H, Albashrawi MA, Al-Busaidi AS, Balakrishnan J, Barlette Y, Basu S, Bose I, Brooks L, Buhalis D, Carter L, Chowdhury S, Crick T, Cunningham SW, Davies GH, Davison RM, De R, Dennehy D, Duan YQ, Dubey R, Dwivedi R, Edwards JS, Flavian C, Gauld R, Grover V, Hu MC, Janssen M, Jones P, Junglas I, Khorana S, Kraus S, Larsen KR, Latreille P, Laumer S, Malik FT, Mardani A, Mariani M, Mithas S, Mogaji E,

Nord JH, O'Commor S, Okumus F, Pagani M, Pandey N, Papagiannidis S, Pappas IO, Pathak N, Pries-Heje J, Raman R, Rana NP, Rehm SV, Ribeiro-Navarrete S, Richter A, Rowe F, Sarker S, Stahl NC, Tiwari MK, van der Aalst W, Venkatesh V, Viglia G, Wade M, Walton P, Wirtz J, Wright R (2023) So what if ChatGPT wrote it? Multidisciplinary perspectives on opportunities, challenges and implications of generative conversational AI for research, practice and policy. Int J Inf Manag 71(102642):1–63

Elliot S, Webster J (2017) Editorial: special issue on empirical research on information systems addressing the challenges of environmental sustainability: an imperative for urgent action. Inf Syst J 27(4):367–378

Elmore SA, Weston EA (2020) Predatory journals: what they are and how to avoid them. Toxicol Pathol 48(4):607–610

Gaskin J, Lowry PB, Hull D (2016) Leveraging multimedia to advance science by disseminating a greater variety of scholarly contributions in more accessible formats. J Assoc Inf Syst 17(6):413–434

Gioia DA, Pitre E (1990) Multi-paradigm perspective on theory building. Acad Manag Rev 15(4):584–602

Gioia DA, Corley KG, Hamilton AL (2013) Seeking qualitative rigor in inductive research. Organ Res Methods 16(1):15–31

Green SE, Li Y, Nohria N (2009) Suspended in self-spun webs of significance: a rhetorical model of institutionalization and institutionally-embedded agency. Acad Manag J 52(1):11–36

Gregor S (2006) The nature of theory in information systems. MIS Q 30(3):611–642

Halverson CA (2004) The value of persistence: A study of the creation, ordering and use of conversation archives by a knowledge worker. In: Proceedings of the 37th Hawaii international conference on system sciences, p 1–10

Hardin AM, Fuller M, Davison RM (2007) I know I can, but can we? Culture and efficacy beliefs in global virtual teams. Small Group Res 38(1):1–26

Huang Q, Davison RM, Gu JB (2008) Impact of personal and cultural factors on knowledge sharing in China. Asia Pac J Manag 25(3):451–471

Ingold T (2013) Making: anthropology, archaeology, art and architecture. Routledge, London

Jarvenpaa SL, Majchrzak A (2008) Knowledge collaboration among professionals protecting national security: role of transactive memories in ego-centered knowledge networks. Organ Sci 19(2):260–276

Kaplan R, Norton D (1992) The balanced scorecard – measures that drive performance. Harv Bus Rev 70(1):71–79

Lee AS (1995) Reviewing a manuscript for publication. J Oper Manag 13(1):87–92

Lee JS, Pries-Heje J, Baskerville RL (2011) Theorizing in design science research. In: Jain H, Sinha AP, Vitharana P (eds) Proceedings of the 6th international conference DESRIST service-oriented perspectives in design science research. Springer, Berlin, pp 1–16

Lewin K (1945) The research center for group dynamics at Massachusetts Institute of Technology. Sociometry 8(2):126–136

Martinsons MG, Davison RM (2007) Strategic decision making and support systems: comparing American, Chinese and Japanese management. Decis Support Syst 43(1):284–300

Martinsons MG, Davison RM, Tse DSK (1999) The balanced scorecard: a foundation for the strategic management of information systems. Decis Support Syst 25(1):71–88

Martinsons MG, Davison RM, Ou CXJ (2015) Developing a new theory of knowledge sharing: documenting and reflecting on a messy process. 75th AoM conference, Vancouver, August 7–11

Müller SD, Sæbø JI (2024) The 'hijacking' of the Scandinavian journal of information systems: implications for the information systems community. Inf Syst J 34(2):xx–xx

Organ DW (1988) Organizational citizenship behavior: the good soldier syndrome. Lexington Books, Lexington, MA

Ou CXJ, Davison RM (2011) Interactive or interruptive: instant messaging at work. Decis Support Syst 52(1):61–72

Ou CXJ, Pavlou PA, Davison RM (2014) Swift guanxi in online marketplaces: the role of computer-mediated-communication technologies. Manag Inf Syst Q 38(1):209–230

Owen A (2017) Into the grey zone: a neuroscientist explores the border between life and death. Guardian Faber, London

Pagel M (2012) Wired for culture: the natural history of human cooperation. Penguin, Harmondsworth

Tarafdar M, Davison RM (2018) Research in information systems: intra-disciplinary and inter-disciplinary approaches. J AIS 19(6):523–551

Tarafdar M, Davison RM (2020) The art of referencing. Inf Syst J 30(5):787–790

Tarafdar M, Davison RM (2021) The associate editor and senior editor roles at premier IS journals. Inf Syst J 31(4):515–520

Techatassanasoontorn AA, Davison RM (2022) Scholarly conversation through a review response document. Inf Syst J 32(4):691–695

Tim Y, Pan SL, Ractham P, Kaewkitipong L (2017) Digitally enabled disaster response: the emergence of social media as boundary objects in a flooding disaster. Inf Syst J 27(2):197–232

Walsham G (2012) Are we making a better world with ICTs? Reflections on a future agenda for the IS field. J Inf Technol 27(2):87–93

Webster J, Watson RT (2002) Analyzing the past to prepare for the future: writing a literature review. MIS Q 26(2):xiii–xxiii

Weick KE (1989) Theory construction as disciplined imagination. Acad Manag Rev 14(4):516–531

Whetten DA (1989) What constitutes a theoretical contribution? Acad Manag Rev 14(4):490–495

Wolfram D, Wang P, Hembree A, Park H (2020) Open peer review: promoting transparaency in open science. Scientometrics 125:1033–1051

Zheng YQ, Yu A (2016) Affordances of social media in collective action: the case of free lunch for children in China. Inf Syst J 26(3):289–313

GPSR Compliance
The European Union's (EU) General Product Safety Regulation (GPSR) is a set of rules that requires consumer products to be safe and our obligations to ensure this.

If you have any concerns about our products, you can contact us on

ProductSafety@springernature.com

In case Publisher is established outside the EU, the EU authorized representative is:

Springer Nature Customer Service Center GmbH
Europaplatz 3
69115 Heidelberg, Germany

www.ingramcontent.com/pod-product-compliance
Lightning Source LLC
LaVergne TN
LVHW010343260326
834688LV00036B/847